I0819868

Express Yourself 101

Dancing With Words

VOLUME 1

Selected by

Ana Monnar

Readers Are Leaders U.S.A.

First published by
Readers Are Leaders U.S.A.
July 22, 2005
Revised May 28, 2007

Interior lay-out design by Masha Shubin, InkwaterPress.com

ISBN
0-9768035-2-6
ISBN 13
9780976803522

Express Yourself 101

Dancing With Words

VOLUME 1

Readers Are Leaders U.S.A.
Founded in 2002
Miami, Florida
www.ReadersAreLeadersUSA.net

Dedication

To all of the writers from around the world that contributed to this endeavor and to the world of literacy with thanks.

Table of Contents

Acknowledgment

My special thanks to Zelda Glazer for being the founder of The Writing Institute. Zelda Glazer's presence, knowledge, enthusiasm and charisma will always live on. Thank goodness I was chosen to attend the 2005 session. It gave me a chance to meet her personally. Inspiration, emotions, personal and professional growth took its course.

The yearly sessions have made many educators blossom. In return the activities, exercises, writing experiences and innovative strategies are passed on. The young learners will benefit in future classrooms. The teachers will enhance their students' writing ability and knowledge. Teaching writing will be an adventure.

Prologue

Express Yourself 101 Dancing with Words is an anthology of 101 writers from the past, present and future. Not only will you find a compilation of poems and short stories, you will also notice a biography, interview, facts and/or note from the authors, plus photographs or illustrations for each featured individual.

This anthology offer s poems from across the centuries. All 101 writers have a wide variety of diverse cultures. Each contributor represents unique authorship and array of style. The splendor of writing has survived an eternity and will live on. Reading and writing for pleasure, relaxation, enrichment to body, mind and soul is a gift to all that desire to do so.

The book's first section ***"Past"*** will embody famous greats from previous centuries. The second section ***"Present"*** will feature adult writers from the present. The third section ***"Future"*** will provide young adults and children's writing. Authors in general come in all ages and sizes. The selected writers included in this anthology have a lot to offer to the literary world.

Past

Mark Akenside

(1721-1770)

Mark Akenside was born on November 9, 1721 in Newcastle upon Tyne located in northeast England on the Tyne River north of Leeds. His father was a butcher. Mark Akenside suffered an injury when he was rather young from his dad's chopper. The injury left Mark slightly lame; but thank goodness the disability was mild.

Did you know that Mark Akenside considered becoming a minister? Instead he decided to study medicine and became the queen's doctor. He was best known as a poet, but soon earned a great reputation as a physician.

Mark Akenside died at his home where he resided the last ten years of his life on June 23, 1770. His cause of death was a fever. He was the son of Mark Akenside and Mary Akenside.

Hymn to Science

Science! Thou fair effusive ray
from the great source of mental day,
Free, generous, and refin'd!
Descend with all thy treasures fraught,
Illumine each bewilder'd thought,
and bless my lab' ring mind.

But first with thy resistless light,
Disperse those phantoms from my sight,
Those mimic shades of thee;
The scholiast's learning, sophist's cant,
The visionary bigot's rant,
The monk's philosophy.

O! let thy powerful charms impart
The patient head, the candid heart,
Devoted to thy sway;
Which no weak passions e'er mislead,
Which still with dauntless steps proceed
Where Reason points the way.

Give me to learn each secret cause;
Let number's, figure's, motion's laws
Reveal'd before me stand;
these to great Nature's scenes apply,
and round the globe, and thro' the sky,
Disclose her working hand.

Next, to thy nobler search resigned,
the busy, restless, human mind
Thro' every maze pursue;
Detect Perception where it lies,
Catch the ideas as they rise,
And all their changes view.

Say from what simple springs began
The vast, ambitious thoughts of man,
Which range beyond control;
Which seek Eternity to trace,
Dive thro' the infinity of space,
And strain to grasp the whole.

Her secret stores let Memory tell,
Bid Fancy quit her fairy cell,
In all her colours drest;
While prompt her sallies to control,
Reason, the judge, recalls the soul
To Truth's severest test.

Then launch thro' Being's wide extent;
Let the fair scale, with just ascent,
and cautious steps, be trod;
and from the dead, corporeal mass,
Thro' each progressive order pass
To Instinct, Reason, God.

There, Science! veil thy daring eye;
Nor dive too deep, nor soar too high,
In that divine abyss;
To Faith content thy beams to lend,
Her hopes t' assure, her steps befriend,
And light her way to bliss.

Then downwards take thy flight agen;
Mix with the policies of men,
and social nature's ties:
The plan, the genius of each state,
its interest and its pow'rs relate,
its fortunes and its rise.

Thro' private life pursue thy course,
Trace every action to its source,
And means and motives weigh:
Put tempers, passions in the scale,
Mark what degrees in each prevail,
And fix the doubtful sway.

That last, best effort of thy skill,
to form the life, and rule the will,
propitious pow'r impart:
Teach me to cool my passion's fires,
Make me the judge of my desires,
The master of my heart.

Raise me above the vulgar breath,
Pursuit of fortune, fear of death,
And all in life that's mean.
Still true to reason be my plan,
Still let my action speak the man,
Thro' every various scene.

Hail! Queen of manners, light of truth;
Hail! Charm of age, and guide of youth;
Sweet refuge of distress:
In business, thou! Exact, polite;
Thou giv'st Retirement its delight
Prosperity its grace.

Of wealth, pow'r, freedom, thou!
The cause;
Foundress of order, cities, laws,
of arts inventress, thou!
Without thee what were human kind?
How vast their wants, their thoughts how blind!
Their joys how mean! How few!

Sun of the soul! Thy beams unveil!
Let others spread the daring sail,
On Fortune's faithless sea;
While undiluted, happier I
from the vain tumult timely fly,
and sit in peace with thee.

Mark Akenside

The Pleasures of Imagination

BOOK 1

With what attractive charms this goodly frame
Of Nature touches the consenting hearts
Of mortal men; and what the pleasing stores
Which beauteous imitation thence derives
To deck the poet's, or the painter's toil;
My verse unfolds. Attend; ye gentle pow'rs
of musical delight! And while I sing
your gifts, your honours, dance around my strain.
Thou, smiling queen of every tuneful breast,
Indulgent Fancy! from the fruitful banks
Of Avon, whence thy rosy fingers cull
Fresh flowers and dews to sprinkle on the turf
Where Shakespeare lies, be present: and with thee
Let Fiction come, upon her vagrant wings
Wafting ten thousand colours through the air,
Which, by the glances of her magic eye,
She blends and shifts at will, through countless forms,
Her wild creation. Goddess of the lyre,
which rules the accents of the moving sphere,
Wilt thou, eternal Harmony! Descend
and join this festive train? for with thee comes
The guide, the guardian of their lovely sports,
Majestic Truth; and where Truth deigns to come,
Her sister Liberty will not be far.
Be present all ye genii, who conduct
the wandering footsteps of the youthful bard,
New to your springs and shades: who touch his ear
With finer sounds: who heighten to his eye
The bloom of Nature, and before him turn
The gayest, happiest attitude of things.

Or shall I mention, where celestial Truth
Her awful light discloses, to bestow
a more majestic pomp on Beauty's frame?
For man loves knowledge, and the beams of Truth

More welcome touch his understanding's eye,
Than all the blandishments of sound his ear,
Than all of taste his tongue. Nor ever yet
The melting rainbow's vernal-tinctured hues
To me have shone so pleasing, as when first
The hand of Science pointed out the path
In which the sun-beams gleaming from the west
Fall on the watery cloud, whose darksome veil
Involves the orient; and that trickling shower
Piercing through every crystalline convex
Of clustering dew-drops to their flight oppos'd,
Recoil at length where concave all behind
The internal surface on each glassy orb
Repeals their forward passage into air;
That thence direct they seek the radiant goal
From which their course began; and, as they strike
In different lines the gazer's obvious eye,
Assume a different lustre, through the brede
Of colours changing from the splendid rose
To the pale violet's dejected hue.

Mark Akenside

Elizabeth Barrett Browning

(1806-1861)

One thing this author shares with me is her birthday. We were both born on March 6th. The only thing that is different is the year of birth. In her case the year of birth was 1806. Elizabeth Moulton-Barrett was born in Durham, England. Elizabeth was the eldest of 12 siblings.

Elizabeth's father was very wealthy. Most of his fortune was made from Jamaican sugar plantations that were worked by slaves. Elizabeth's father did not want any of his one dozen children married. Imagine that! He married and had all of those children. I guess with him it must have been, "Do as I say and not as I do." Elizabeth was home schooled and learned many languages including Latin, Greek and Portuguese. Her dad had her first poem published when she was 13 years old.

Poor Elizabeth had an abundance of consequences sequencing her life. Her brothers were sent away to get an education, she had problems with her lungs, fever, ailments and loneliness. After that her mother died, and then some of her brothers started dying also. She was left behind and she would submerge herself to writing poems.

Subsequently some of the family's fortune was lost due to the freedom of slaves and the family home had to be sold. Elizabeth Barrett became a reputable, well-known poet and met a man named Robert. Robert Browning was a famous poet and when he read Elizabeth's poems, he was impressed and wrote to her. They would secretly correspond due to her father's selfishness. Her dad did not approve of their courtship nor would he allow marriage. So guess what, Elizabeth and Robert eloped. Yes, they ran away and secretly got married. Her father totally disowned her and refused further communications since 1846 when they wedded.

Elizabeth Barrett-Browning and Robert Browning moved to Florence, Italy. This helped Elizabeth's lungs condition tremendously. The air was much clearer than in England, therefore improving her breathing and health. Elizabeth and Robert Browning had one son. When she died June 29, 1861, Elizabeth was only 55 years old. Her husband and son moved back to England after her death.

The man in my opinion was not a very nice man. He should have learned from the following quotation, by Abraham Lincoln, *"Whenever I hear anyone arguing for slavery, I feel a strong impulse to see it tried on him personally."* Plus my own quotation, Ana Monnar, "When we bleed, we bleed the same color." What I mean is that, we are all children of the same creator. We all have a heart, feelings and self-worth. Decisions we make throughout our lives play a key role. Race creed and color does not make one better or worse than the next person.

The Autumn

Go, sit upon the lofty hill,
and turn your eyes around,
where waving woods and waters wild
do hymn an autumn sound.
The summer sun is faint on them –
The summer flowers depart –
Sit still – as all transform'd to stone,
except your musing heart.

How there you sat in summer-time,
May yet be in your mind;
and how you heard the green woods sing
beneath the freshening wind.
Though the same wind now blows around,
you would its blast recall;
for every breath that stirs the trees,
doth cause a leaf to fall.

Oh! Like that wind, is all the mirth
that flesh and dust impart:
We cannot bear its visiting,
when change is on the heart.
Gay words and jests may make us smile,
When Sorrow is asleep;
but other things must make us smile,
When Sorrow bids us weep!

The dearest hands that clasp our hands
Their presence may be o'er;
The dearest voice that meets our ear,
That tone may come no more!
Youth fades; and then, the joys of youth,
Which once refresh'd our mind,
Shall come – as, on those sighing woods,
The chilling autumn wind.

Hear not the wind – view not the woods;
Look out o'er vale and hill –
In spring, the sky encircled them –
The sky is round them still.
Come autumn's scathe – come winter's cold –
Come change – and human fate!
Whatever prospect Heaven doth bound,
Can ne'er be desolate.

Elizabeth Barrett Browning

How Do I Love Thee?

How do I love thee?
Let me count the ways.
I love thee to the depth
and breadth
and height
my soul can reach,
when feeling out of sight.
For the ends of Being and ideal Grace
I love thee to the level of every day's
most quiet need,
by sun and candlelight.
I love thee freely,
as men strive for Right;
I love thee purely,
as they turn from Praise.
I love thee with the passion
put to use in my old grief,
and with my childhood's faith.
I love thee with a love I seemed to lose
with my lost saints;
I love thee with the breath, Smiles, tears,
of all my life!
And, if God choose,
I shall but love thee better after death.

Elizabeth Barrett Browning

William Blake

(1757-1827)

William Blake was an English poet, engraver and painter. He was born in London, England. His talents were evident since early age. William Blake's first treasury of poems was published in 1783. The book was titled, *Poetical Sketches*. Blake married Catherine and both stayed married until his death.

Works by William Blake are many. Some include the following poems titled, *A Poison Tree, Africa, Holy Thursday, Infant Sorrow, Introduction to Songs of Innocence, Love's Secret, Songs of Experience, The Chimney Sweeper, The Little Boy, The Tiger, To See the World,* plus many more.

The Divine Image

To Mercy, Pity, Peace, and Love
All pray in their distress;
And to these virtues of delight
Return their thankfulness.
For Mercy, Pity, Peace, and Love
Is God, our father dear,
And Mercy, Pity, Peace, and Love
Is Man, his child and care.
For Mercy has a human heart,
Pity a human face,
And Love, the human form divine,
And Peace, the human dress
Then every man, of every clime,
That prays in his distress,
Prays to the human form divine,
Love, Mercy, Pity, Peace
And all must love the human form,
In heathen, Turk, or Jew;
Where Mercy, Love, & Pity dwell
There God is dwelling too.

WILLIAM BLAKE

To See the World

To see the world in a grain of sand,
And Heaven in a wild flower,
Hold infinity in the palm of your hand
and eternity in an hour
He who binds himself to a joy
Does the winged life destroy
He who kisses joy as it flies
Lives in eternity's sunrise

William Blake

The Little Black Boy

My mother bore me in the southern wild,
and I am black, but oh my soul is white!
White as an angel is the English child,
but I am black, as if bereaved of light.
My mother taught me underneath a tree,
and, sitting down before the heat of day,
she took me on her lap and kissed me,
and, pointed to the east, began to say:
"Look on the rising sun: there God does live,
and gives His light, and gives His heat away,
And flowers and trees and beasts and men receive
Comfort in morning, joy in the noonday.
"And we are put on earth a little space,
that we may learn to bear the beams of love
And these black bodies and this sun burnt face
Is but a cloud, and like a shady grove.

William Blake

Robert Browning

(1812-1889)

Robert Browning was born on May 7, 1812 in Camberwell, England. He was the son of Robert Browning Senior and Sarah Anna Wiedemann. His mother was a pianist and his father was a banker and was recognized for owning a collection of more than 6,000 rare books. Most of Robert Browning's education was self taught by reading an abundance of the books in his father's collection. He married Elizabeth Barrett Browning.

Another one of my quotes goes as follows, "It goes to show you that those who wish to learn gain knowledge regardless the barriers of poverty, opportunity or status." **Ana Monnar**

My Last Duchess

FERRARA

That's my last Duchess painted on the wall,
Looking as if she were alive. I call
that piece a wonder, now: Fr Pandolf's hands
Worked busily a day, and there she stands.
Will't please you sit and look at her? I said
"Fr Pandolf" by design, for never read
Strangers like you that pictured countenance,
The depth and passion of its earnest glance,
But to myself they turned (since none puts by
The curtain I have drawn for you, but I)
And seemed as they would ask me, if they durst,
How such a glance came there; so, not the first
Are you to turn and ask thus. Sir, 'twas not
Her husband's presence only, called that spot
Of joy into the Duchess' cheek: perhaps
Fr Pandolf chanced to say, "Her mantle laps
Over my lady's wrist too much," or "Paint"
"Must never hope to reproduce the faint
Half-flush that dies along her throat:" such stuff
Was courtesy, she thought, and cause enough
For calling up that spot of joy. She had
a heart - how shall I say? - Too soon made glad,
too easily impressed; she liked whate'er
she looked on, and her looks went everywhere.
Sir, 'twas all one My favour at her breast,
The dropping of the daylight in the West,
The bough of cherries some officious fool
Broke in the orchard for her, the white mule
She rode with round the terrace – all and each
Would draw from her alike the approving speech,
Or blush, at least. She thanked men, – good! But thanked
somehow - I know not how – as if she ranked
my gift of a nine-hundred – years – old name
with anybody's gift. Who'd stoop to blame
this sort of trifling? Even had you skill

In speech – (which I have not) - to make your will
Quite clear to such one, and say, "Just this" Or that in you disgusts me;
here you miss, "Or there exceed the mark" - and if she let
Herself be lessoned so, nor plainly set
Her wits to yours, forsooth, and made excuse
E'en then would be some stooping; and I choose
Never to stoop. Oh sir, she smiled, no doubt,
when're I passed her; but who passed without
much the same smile? This grew; I gave commands;
then all smiles stopped together. There she stands
As if alive. Will't please you rise? We'll meet
The Company below, then. I repeat,
The Count your master's known munificence
Is ample warrant that no just pretence
Of mine for dowry will be disallowed;
Though his fair daughter's self, as I avowed
At starting, is my object. Nay, we'll go
Together down, sir. Notice Neptune, though,
Taming a sea-horse, thought a rarity,
Which Claus of Innsbruck cast in bronze for me!

Robert Browning

Women and Roses

I.

I dream of a red-rose tree.
And which of its roses three
Is the dearest rose to me?

II.

Round and round, like a dance of snow
In a dazzling drift, as its guardians, go
Floating the women faded for ages,
Sculptured in stone, on the poet's pages
Then follow women fresh and gay,
Living and loving and loved to-day
Last, in the rear, flee the multitude of maidens,
Beauties yet unborn; and all, to one cadence,
They circle their rose on my rose tree.

III.

Dear rose, thy term is reached,
Thy leaf hangs loose and bleached:
Bees pass it un-impeached

IV.

Stay then, stoop, since I cannot climb,
You, great shapes of the antique time!
How shall I fix you, fire you, freeze you,
Break my heart at your feet to please you?
Oh, to possess and be possessed!
Hearts that beat 'neath each pallid breast!
Once but of love, the poesy, the passion,
Drink but once and die! – In vain, the same fashion,
They circle their rose on my rose tree.

V.

Dear rose, thy joys undimmed,
Thy cup is ruby-rimmed,
Thy cup's heart nectar-brimmed

VI.

Deep, as drops from a statue's plinth
The bee sucked in by the hyacinth,
So will I bury me while burning
Quench like him at a plunge my yearning,
Eyes in your eyes, lips on your lips!
Fold me fast where the cincture slips,
Prison all my soul in eternities of pleasure,
Girdle me for once! But no – the old measure,
They circle their rose on my rose tree.

VII.

Dear rose without a thorn,
Thy bud's the babe unborn:
First streak of a new morn

VIII.

Wings, lend wings for the cold, the clear!
What is far conquers what is near.
Roses will bloom nor want beholders,
Sprung from the dust where our flesh molders.
What shall arrive with the cycle's change?
A novel grace and a beauty strange
I will make an Eve, be the artist that began her,
Shaped her to his mind! – Alas! In like manner
They circle their rose on my rose tree.

Robert Browning

William Cullen Bryant

(1794–1878)

William Cullen Bryant was born on November 3, 1794, in Cummington, Massachusetts and died on June 12, 1878, in New York City, New York. He wanted to study law in Harvard University, but his father would not give in to that luxury. William Cullen Bryant was determined to get trained in law. So he went about it from much more modest means.

William Cullen Bryant wrote "Thenatopsis" before he was 21 years old. William Cullen Bryant was a poet and newspaper editor. Later he was known and respected as a poet and became part owner and editor in chief of the New York, *Evening Post.*

William Cullen Bryant started writing poetry as a source of income. Later on in life he wrote poems as a hobby. As a columnist, he was in favor of free speech and the elimination of slavery. He abandoned the frequency of poetry writing to pursue being one of the largest advocates for the abolition of slavery.

Thanatopsis

To him who in the love of nature holds
Communion with her visible forms, she speaks
A various language; for his gayer hours
She has a voice of gladness, and a smile
and eloquence of beauty; and she glides
Into his darker musings, with a mild
And healing sympathy that steals away
Their sharpness ere he is aware. When thoughts
Of the last bitter hour come like a blight
Over thy spirit, and sad images
Of the stern agony, and shroud, and pall,
And breathless darkness, and the narrow house,
Make thee to shudder, and grow sick at heart;
Go forth, under the open sky, and list
To Nature's teachings, while from all around
Earth and her waters, and the depths of air –
Comes a still voice. Yet a few days, and thee
The all-beholding sun shall see no more
In all his course; nor yet in the cold ground,
Where thy pale form was laid, with many tears,
Nor in the embrace of ocean, shall exist
Thy image. Earth, that nourished thee, shall claim
Thy growth, to be resolved to earth again,
And, lost each human trace, surrendering up
Thine individual being, shalt thou go
To mix forever with the elements,
To be a brother to the insensible rock
And to the sluggish clod, which the rude swain
Turns with his share, and treads upon. The oak
shall send his roots abroad, and pierce thy mold.

Yet not to thine eternal resting-place
shalt thou retire alone, nor couldst thou wish
Couch more magnificent. Thou shalt lie down
With patriarchs of the infant world – with kings,
The powerful of the earth – the wise, the good,

Fair forms, and hoary seers of ages past,
All in one mighty sepulcher. The hills
Rock-ribbed and ancient as the sun – he vales
Stretching in pensive quietness between;
The venerable woods – rivers that move
In majesty, and the complaining brooks
That make the meadows green; and, poured round all,
Old Ocean's gray and melancholy waste,
Are but the solemn decorations all
Of the great tomb of man. The golden sun,
The planets, all the infinite host of heaven,
Are shining on the sad abodes of death
Through the still lapse of ages. All that tread
the globe are but a handful to the tribes
that slumber in its bosom. – Take the wings
Of morning, pierce the Barchan's wilderness,
Or lose thyself in the continuous woods
Where rolls the Oregon, and hears no sound,
Save his own dashing – yet the dead are there:
And millions in those solitudes, since first
The flight of years began, have laid them down
In their last sleep – the dead reign there alone.

So shalt thou rest – and what if thou withdraw
In silence from the living, and no friend
Take note of thy departure? All that breathe
will share thy destiny. The gay will laugh
when thou art gone, the solemn brood of care
Plod on, and each one as before will chase
His favorite phantom; yet all these shall leave
their mirth and their employments, and shall come
and make their bed with thee. As the long train
Of ages glides away, the sons of men –
The youth in life's fresh spring, and he who goes
In the full strength of years, matron and maid,
The speechless babe, and the gray-headed man –
Shall one by one be gathered to thy side,
By those, who in their turn, shall follow them.

So live, that when thy summons comes to join
The innumerable caravan, which moves
To that mysterious realm, where each shall take
His chamber in the silent halls of death,
Thou go not, like the quarry-slave at night,
Scourged to his dungeon, but, sustained and soothed
By an unfaltering trust, approach thy grave
Like one who wraps the drapery of his couch
About him, and lies down to pleasant dreams

WILLIAM CULLEN BRYANT
Written when he was 16 years old

Charles Dickens

(1812-1870)

Charles Dickens was born on February 7th, 1812 and died June 9th, 1870. Dickens was a poet during the Victorian Literary Period. He was also a novelist and journalist. Some of his famous works consisted of; *A Christmas Carol, David Copperfield, Hard Times, Oliver Twist,* and *A Tale of Two Cities.* He married Catherine Hogarth Dickens on April 2nd, 1836. Charles Dickens and Catherine Hogarth Dickens separated in 1858 after conceiving ten children.

A Child's Hymn

Hear my prayer, O heavenly Father,
ere I lay me down to sleep;
Bid Thy angels, pure and holy,
Round my bed their vigil keep.

My sins are heavy, but Thy mercy
Far outweighs them, every one;
Down before Thy cross I cast them,
Trusting in Thy help alone.

Keep me through this night of peril
Underneath its boundless shade;
Take me to Thy rest, I pray Thee,
When my pilgrimage is made.

None shall measure out Thy patience
By the span of human thought;
None shall bind the tender mercies
Which Thy Holy Son has bought.

Pardon all my past transgressions,
Give me strength for days to come;
Guide and guard me with Thy blessing
Till Thy angels bid me home.

Charles Dickens

Eugene Field

(1850 -1895)

Eugene Field was born in Saint Louis, Missouri on September 2, 1850 and died on November 4, 1895 at the age of 45. He was raised by his cousin in Massachusetts after the death of his mother. Eugene Field became known for children's poetry and humorous essays.

Field attempted law school and acting but was unsuccessful. He also attended quite a few colleges, but did not take his studies seriously. He was known to be a joker and loved to pull pranks. After going to Europe and returning to the United States of America he was broke.

He then started working. Eugene Field worked as a journalist for *The Gazette* in St. Joseph Missouri in 1875. He soon was promoted to editor in *The Gazette.* He married Julia Comstock in 1875 and they had eight children.

Later on Field moved to Kansas City, Missouri, and then Denver, Colorado, followed to Chicago, Illinois. His career as an editorial writer and managing editor proved to be successful. Publishing his poetry started as a side job and in 1879 his book *Christian Treasures* went live. Numerous other titles followed and Eugene Field became well known.

Little Boy Blue

The little toy dog is covered with dust,
But sturdy and stanch he stands;
And the little toy soldier is red with rust,
And his musket moulds in his hands.
Time was when the little toy dog was new,
and the soldier was passing fair;
and that was the time when our Little Boy Blue
Kissed them and put them there.
"Now, don't you go till I come," he said,
"And don't you make any noise!"
So, toddling off to his trundle-bed,
He dreamt of the pretty toys;
and, as he was dreaming, an angel song
awakened our Little Boy Blue –
Oh! The years are many, the years are long,
But the little toy friends are true!
Ay, faithful to Little Boy Blue they stand,
Each in the same old place –
Awaiting the touch of a little hand,
The smile of a little face;
And they wonder, as waiting the long years through
In the dust of that little chair,
What has become of our Little Boy Blue,
Since he kissed them and put them there.

EUGENE FIELD

The Three Kings of Cologne

From out Cologne there came three kings
To worship Jesus Christ, their King
To Him they sought fine herbs they brought,
And many a beauteous golden thing;
They brought their gifts to Bethlehem town,
And in that manger set them down.

Then spoke the first king and he said:
O Child, most heavenly, bright, and fair!
I bring this crown to Bethlehem town
For Thee, and only Thee, to wear;
So give a heavenly crown to me
When I shall come at last to Thee!

The second, then – I bring Thee here
This royal robe, O Child!" he cried;
Of silk't is spun, and such an one
There is not in the world beside;
So in the day of doom requite
Me with a heavenly robe of white!

The third king gave his gift, and quoth:
Spikenard and myrrh to Thee I bring,
And with these twain would I most fain
Anoint the body of my King;
So may their incense sometime rise
To plead for me in yonder skies!

Thus spoke the three kings of Cologne,
That gave their gifts and went their way;
And now kneel I in prayer hard by
The cradle of the Child to-day;
Nor crown, nor robe, nor spice I bring
As offering unto Christ, my King

Yet have I brought a gift the Child
May not despise, however small;
For here I lay my heart today,
And it is full of love to all.
Take Thou the poor but loyal thing,
My only tribute, Christ, my King!

Eugene Field

Robert Frost

(1874 – 1963)

Did you know that Robert Frost was a four time winner of the Pulitzer Prize? The Pulitzer Prize is a United States award considered as the highest honor in print journalism. This award also honors literary achievements and musical compositions.

Robert Lee Frost was born on March 26, 1874 in San Francisco, California. Robert Frost was a poet well known for free verse, rhythm and meter, traditional and experimental poetry. Robert Frost's father died when he was 11 years old. He went to college, was also a teacher, then a reporter and an editor for a newspaper. He married Elinor White. He recited his work, *"The Gift Outright"* at the inauguration of President John F. Kennedy in 1961.

A Prayer in Spring

Oh, give us pleasure in the flowers today;
And give us not to think so far away
As the uncertain harvest; keep us here
All simply in the springing of the year

Oh, give us pleasure in the orchard white,
Like nothing else by day, like ghosts by night;
And make us happy in the happy bees,
The swarms dilating round the perfect trees.

And make us happy in the darting bird
That suddenly above the bees is heard,
The meteor that thrusts in with needle bill,
And off a blossom in mid air stands still.

For this is love and nothing else is love,
To which it is reserved for God above
To sanctify to what far ends he will,
But which it only needs that we fulfill

Robert Frost

Evening in a Sugar Orchard

From where I lingered in a lull in March
Outside the sugar-house one night for choice,
I called the fireman with a careful voice
And bade him leave the pan and stoke the arch:
'O fireman, give the fire another stoke,
And send more sparks up chimney with the smoke.'
I thought a few might tangle, as they did,
Among bare maple boughs, and in the rare
Hill atmosphere not cease to glow,
And so be added to the moon up there.
The moon, though slight, was moon enough to show
On every tree a bucket with a lid,
And on black ground a bear-skin rug of snow.
The sparks made no attempt to be the moon.
They were content to figure in the trees
As Leo, Orion, and the Pleiades
And that was what the boughs were full of soon.

Robert Frost

The Road Not Taken

Two roads diverged in a yellow wood,
And sorry I could not travel both
And be one traveler, long I stood
And looked down one as far as I could
To where it bent in the undergrowth;
Then took the other, as just as fair,
And having perhaps the better claim,
Because it was grassy and wanted wear;
Though as for that the passing there
Had worn them really about the same,
And both that morning equally lay
In leaves no step had trodden black.
Oh, I kept the first for another day!
Yet knowing how way leads on to way,
I doubted if I should ever come back.
I shall be telling this with a sigh
Somewhere ages and ages hence:
Two roads diverged in a wood, and I –
I took the one less traveled by,
And that has made all the difference.

ROBERT FROST

Samuel Johnson

(1709-1784)

Samuel Johnson was born in Lichfield, England on September 18, 1709 and died on December 13, 1784. His biggest achievement was being the author of *A Dictionary of the English Language* written in 1755.

Michael and Sarah Johnson were Samuel's parents. Samuel Johnson was the son of a bookseller. He also had one brother named, Nathaniel Johnson. Samuel Johnson married Elizabeth Porter Johnson on July 9, 1735. Johnson also wrote poems, essays and plays. He spoke English, Greek and Latin.

Samuel Johnson suffered from more than a good share if illnesses such as asthma, emphysema of the lungs, gout, granular disease of the kidneys, hypochondria, scrofula and suffered a severe stroke.

One and Twenty

Long-expected one and twenty
Ling' ring year at last has flown,
Pomp and pleasure, pride and plenty
Great Sir John, are all your own.
Loosen'd from the minor's tether,
Free to mortgage or to sell,
Wild as wind, and light as feather
Bid the slaves of thrift farewell.
Call the Betties, Kates, and Jennies
Ev'ry name that laughs at care,
Lavish of your Grandsire's guineas,
Show the spirit of an heir.
All that prey on vice and folly
Joy to see their quarry fly,
Here the gamester light and jolly
There the lender grave and sly.
Wealth, Sir John, was made to wander,
Let it wander as it will;
See the jockey, see the pander,
Bid them come, and take their fill.
When the bonny blade carouses,
Pockets full, and spirits high,
What are acres? What are houses?
Only dirt, or wet or dry
If the Guardian or the Mother
Tell the woes of willful waste,
Scorn their counsel and their pother,
You can hang or drown at last.

SAMUEL JOHNSON

John Keats

(1795-1821)

John Keats was born on October 31, 1795. He was the son of Thomas Keats and Frances Keats. He had two brothers George Keats and Thomas Keats. He also had one sister named Frances Mary Llanos. He spoke English, Latin and Italian.

John Keats first published book was title, *Poems*. It was sad that one of his brothers died of tuberculosis and John Keats suffered from tuberculosis also. Keats was only 25 years old when he died.

If by Dull Rhymes Our English Must be Chained

If by dull rhymes our English must be chained,
And, like Andromeda, the Sonnet sweet
Fettered, in spite of pained loveliness;
Let us find out, if we must be constrained,
Sandals more interwoven and complete
To fit the naked foot of poesy;
Let us inspect the lyre, and weigh the stress
Of every chord, and see what may be gained
By ear industrious, and attention meet;
Misers of sound and syllable, no less
Than Midas of his coinage, let us be
Jealous of dead leaves in the bay wreath crown;
So, if we may not let the Muse be free,
She will be bound with garlands of her own.

John Keats

To the Nile

Son of the old Moon-mountains African!
Chief of the Pyramid and Crocodile!
We call thee fruitful, and that very while
A desert fills our seeing's inward span:
Nurse of swart nations since the world began,
Art thou so fruitful? Or dost thou beguile
Such men to honour thee, who, worn with toil,
Rest for a space 'twixt Cairo and Decan?
O may dark fancies err! They surely do;
'Tis ignorance that makes a barren waste
of all beyond itself. Thou dost bedew
Green rushes like our rivers, and dost taste
the pleasant sunrise. Green isles hast thou too,
And to the sea as happily dost haste.

JOHN KEATS

Amy Lowell

(1874 – 1925)

Amy Lowell was born on February 9, 1874 and died on May 12, 1925. She was an American poet who won the Pulitzer Prize for Poetry in 1926 a year after she died. Amy Lowell became a poet once she reached her adult years. As a young girl she attended private schools. Her family was very wealthy and would not consent to Amy Lowell getting a formal education from any university. Therefore she took the initiative to educate herself through the 7,000 volume library her father owned.

Amy Lowell's brother, Percival Lowell was the famous astronomer. He predicted the existence of the planet Pluto. Good genes were in her family tree because her other brother, Abbott Lawrence Lowell was the President of Harvard University.

Amy Lowell met Ada Dwyer Russell, an actress and widow. Ada was 11 years older than Amy and both lived and traveled together until Amy Lowell's death. Her cause of death was from a cerebral hemorrhage.

Azure and Gold

April had covered the hills
With flickering yellows and reds,
The sparkle and coolness of snow
Was blown from the mountain beds
Across a deep-sunken stream
The pink of blossoming trees,
And from windless apple blooms
The humming of many bees
The air was of rose and gold
Arabesque with the song of birds
Who, swinging unseen under leaves,
Made music more eager than words
Of a sudden, aslant the road,
A brightness to dazzle and stun,
A glint of the bluest blue,
A flash from a sapphire sun
Blue-birds so blue,'t was a dream,
An impossible, un-conceived hue,
The high sky of summer dropped down
Some rapturous ocean to woo
Such a colour, such infinite light!
The heart of a fabulous gem,
Many-faceted, brilliant and rare
Centre Stone of the earth's diadem!
Centre Stone of the Crown of the World,
"Sincerity" graved on your youth!
And your eyes hold the blue-bird flash,
The sapphire shaft, which is truth

AMY LOWELL

Patterns

I walk down the garden paths,
and all the daffodils
Are blowing, and the bright blue squills.
I walk down the patterned garden-paths
in my stiff, brocaded gown.
With my powdered hair and jeweled fan,
I too am a rare
Pattern. As I wander down
the garden paths.
My dress is richly figured,
and the train
makes a pink and silver stain
on the gravel, and the thrift
of the borders.
Just a plate of current fashion,
tripping by in high-heeled, ribbon shoes
not a softness anywhere about me,
only whalebone and brocade
And I sink on a seat in the shade
of a lime tree. For my passion
Wars against the stiff brocade
the daffodils and squills
flutter in the breeze
as they please.
And I weep;
for the lime-tree is in blossom
and one small flower has dropped upon my bosom.
And the plashing of water drops
in the marble fountain
comes down the garden-paths.
The dripping never stops.
Underneath my stiffened gown
Is the softness of a woman bathing in a marble basin,
A basin in the midst of hedges grown
So thick, she cannot see her lover hiding,
But she guesses he is near,

And the sliding of the water
Seems the stroking of a dear
Hand upon her.
What is summer in a fine brocaded gown!
I should like to see it lying in a heap upon the ground.
All the pink and silver crumpled up on the ground.
I would be the pink and silver as I ran along the paths,
And he would stumble after,
Bewildered by my laughter.
I should see the sun flashing from his sword-hilt and the buckles on his shoes.
I would choose
To lead him in a maze along the patterned paths,
A bright and laughing maze for my heavy-booted lover,
Till he caught me in the shade,
And the buttons of his waistcoat bruised my body as he clasped me,
Aching, melting, unafraid.
With the shadows of the leaves and the sun drops,
And the plopping of the water drops,
All about us in the open afternoon —
I am very like to swoon
With the weight of this brocade,
For the sun sifts through the shade.
Underneath the fallen blossom
In my bosom,
Is a letter I have hid.
It was brought to me this morning by a rider from the Duke.
"Madam, we regret to inform you that Lord Hartwell
Died in action Thursday se'nnight."
As I read it in the white, morning sunlight,
The letters squirmed like snakes.
"Any answer, Madam," said my footman.
"No," I told him.
"See that the messenger takes some refreshment.
No, no answer."
And I walked into the garden,
Up and down the patterned paths,
In my stiff, correct brocade.
The blue and yellow flowers stood up proudly in the sun,
each one.

I stood upright too,
Held rigid to the pattern
By the stiffness of my gown.
Up and down I walked,
Up and down.
In a month he would have been my husband.
In a month, here, underneath this lime,
We would have broke the pattern;
He for me, and I for him,
He as Colonel, I as Lady,
On this shady seat.
He had a whim
that sunlight carried blessing.
And I answered, "It shall be as you have said,"
Now he is dead.
In summer and in winter I shall walk
Up and down
the patterned garden-paths
in my stiff, brocaded gown.
The squills and daffodils
will give place to pillared roses, and to asters, and to snow.
I shall go
Up and down,
in my gown.
Gorgeously arrayed,
Boned and stayed.
And the softness of my body will be guarded from embrace
by each button, hook, and lace.
For the man who should loose me is dead,
Fighting with the Duke in Flanders,
In a pattern called a war.
Christ! What are patterns for?

Amy Lowell

Edgar Allan Poe

(1809-1849)

Edgar Allan Poe was born on January 19, 1809 in Boston, Massachusetts. His father an actor, David Poe Jr. died approximately in 1810 and his mother an actress, Elizabeth Hopkins Poe in 1811. He was left an orphan when he was very young. He had a brother and sister where all three children were raised by John and Fanny Allan in Richmond, Virginia.

Edgar Allan Poe experienced more hard luck when he was expelled from the University of Virginia in 1926 for not paying gambling debts. He joined the Army, where only a year later in 1927 he was dishonorably discharged for being neglectful to his duties.

Edgar Allan Poe married his 13 year old cousin Virginia Clemm. She became ill and an invalid from a problem of a blood vessel that ruptured. She died a few years later from tuberculosis. That triggered Edgar Allan Poe to a life of using drugs and drinking alcoholic beverages. In 1849 Poe addressed his poem titled, *Annabel Lee* in loving memory to his wife.

Edgar Allan Poe was brilliant and creative. He is well known for his poems and short stories. Yet his life was full of struggles from the time he was a toddler to the time of his death. During the last years of his life Poe suffered from depression, madness and even attempted suicide a year before his death.

Annabel Lee

It was many and many a year ago,
In a kingdom by the sea,
That a maiden there lived whom you may know
By the name of; Annabel Lee –
And this maiden she lived with no other thought
Than to love and be loved by me
She was a child and I was a child,
In this kingdom by the sea,
But we loved with a love that was more than love –
I and my Annabel Lee –
With a love that the winged seraphs of heaven
Coveted her and me

And this was the reason that, long ago,
In this kingdom by the sea,
A wind blew out of a cloud by night
Chilling my Annabel Lee;
So that her high-born kinsman came
And bore her away from me,
To shut her up in a sepulcher
In this kingdom by the sea

The angels, not half so happy in Heaven,
Went envying her and me:
Yes! That was the reason (as all men know,
in this kingdom by the sea)
That the wind came out of a cloud, chilling
And killing my Annabel Lee

But our love it was stronger by far than the love
Of those who were older than we –
Of many far wiser than we –
And neither the angels in Heaven above,
Nor the demons down under the sea,
Can ever dissever my soul from the soul
Of the beautiful Annabel Lee

For the moon never beams without bringing me dreams
Of the beautiful Annabel Lee;
And the stars never rise but I see the bright eyes
Of the beautiful Annabel Lee;
And so, all the night-tide, I lie down by the side
Of my darling, my darling, my life and my bride,
In her sepulcher there by the sea –
In her tomb by the side of the sea

EDGAR ALLAN POE

The Raven

Once upon a midnight dreary, while I pondered, weak and weary,
Over many a quaint and curious volume of forgotten lore –
While I nodded, nearly napping, suddenly there came a tapping,
As of some one gently rapping, rapping at my chamber door.
'Tis some visitor, "I muttered, "tapping at my chamber door –
Only this and nothing more."

Ah, distinctly I remember it was in the bleak December,
and each separate dying ember wrought its ghost upon the floor.
Eagerly I wished the morrow – vainly I had sought to borrow
From my books surcease of sorrow—sorrow for the lost Lenore –
For the rare and radiant maiden whom the angels name Lenore –
Nameless here for evermore.

And the silken sad uncertain rustling of each purple curtain
Thrilled me – filled me with fantastic terrors never felt before;
So that now, to still the beating of my heart, I stood repeating
"'Tis some visitor entreating entrance at my chamber door –
Some late visitor entreating entrance at my chamber door;
This it is and nothing more."

Presently my soul grew stronger; hesitating then no longer,
"Sir," said I, "or Madam, truly your forgiveness I implore;
But the fact is I was napping, and so gently you came rapping,
And so faintly you came tapping, tapping at my chamber door,
That I scarce was sure I heard you" – here I opened wide the door –
Darkness there and nothing more.

Deep into that darkness peering, long I stood there wondering, fearing,
Doubting, dreaming dreams no mortals ever dared to dream before;
But the silence was unbroken, and the stillness gave no token,
And the only word there spoken was the whispered word, "Lenore?"
This I whispered and an echo murmured back the word, "Lenore!" –
Merely this and nothing more.

Back into the chamber turning, all my sour within me burning,
Soon again I heard a tapping something louder than before.
"Surely," said I, "surely that is something at my window lattice;
Let me see, then, what thereat is and this mystery explore –
Let my heart be still a moment and this mystery explore;
'Tis the wind and nothing more.

Open here I flung the shutter, when, with many a flirt and flutter,
In there stepped a stately Raven of the saintly days of yore.
Not the least obeisance made he; not a minute stopped or stayed he,
But, with mien of lord or lady, perched above my chamber door –
Perched upon a bust of Pallas just above my chamber door –
Perched, and sat, and nothing more.

Then the ebony bird beguiling my sad fancy into smiling,
By the grave and stern decorum of the countenance it wore,
"Though thy crest be shorn and shaven, thou," I said, "art sure no craven,
Ghastly grim and ancient Raven wandering from the Nightly shore –
Tell me what thy lordly name is on the Night's Plutonian shore!"
Quoth the Raven, "Nevermore"

Much I marveled this ungainly fowl to hear discourse so plainly,
Though its answer little meaning – little relevancy bore;
For we cannot help agreeing that no living human being
Ever yet was blessed with seeing bird above his chamber door –
Bird or beast upon the sculptured bust above his chamber door,
With such name as "Nevermore"

But the Raven, sitting lonely on that placid bust, spoke only
That one word, as if its soul in that one word he did outpour
Nothing farther then he uttered; not a feather then he fluttered –
Till I scarcely more than muttered: "Other friends have flown before –
On the morrow he will leave me, as my Hopes have flown before."
Then the bird said "Nevermore"

Startled at the stillness broken by reply so aptly spoken,
"Doubtless," said I, "what it utters is its only stock and store,
Caught from some unhappy master whom unmerciful Disaster
Followed fast and followed faster till his songs one burden bore –
Till the dirges of his Hope that melancholy burden bore
Of 'Never – nevermore'"

But the Raven still beguiling all my sad soul into smiling,
Straight I wheeled a cushioned seat in front of bird and bust and door;
Then, upon the velvet sinking, I betook myself to linking
Fancy unto fancy, thinking what this ominous bird of yore
What this grim, ungainly, ghastly, gaunt, and ominous bird of yore
Meant in croaking "Nevermore."

This I sat engaged in guessing, but no syllable expressing
To the fowl whose fiery eyes now burned into my bosom's core;
This and more I sat divining, with my head at ease reclining
On the cushion's velvet lining that the lamp-light gloated o'er,
But whose velvet violet lining with the lamp-light gloating o'er
She shall press, ah, nevermore!

Then, me thought, the air grew denser, perfumed from an unseen censer
Swung by Seraphim whose foot-falls tinkled on the tufted floor.
"Wretch," I cried, "thy God hath lent thee –
by these angels he hath sent thee
Respite – respite and nepenthe from thy memories of Lenore!
Quaff, oh quaff this kind nepenthe and forget this lost Lenore!"
Quoth the Raven, "Nevermore."

"Prophet!" said I, "thing of evil! – Prophet still, if bird or devil! –
Whether Tempter sent, or whether tempest tossed thee here ashore,
Desolate, yet all undaunted, on this desert land enchanted –
On this home by Horror haunted – tell me truly, I implore—
Is there—is there balm in Gilead? – tell me –tell me, I implore!"
Quoth the Raven, "Nevermore"

"Prophet!" said I, "thing of evil! – Prophet still, if bird or devil!
By that Heaven that bends above us—by that God we both adore –
Tell this soul with sorrow laden if, within the distant Aidenn,
It shall clasp a sainted maiden whom the angels name Lenore –
Clasp a rare and radiant maiden whom the angels name Lenore."
Quoth the Raven, "Nevermore"

"Be that our sign of parting, bird or fiend!" I shrieked, up starting –
"Get thee back into the tempest and the Night's Plutonian shore!
Leave no black plume as a token of that lie thy soul has spoken!
Leave my loneliness unbroken! – quit the bust above my door!
Take thy beak from out my heart, and take thy form from off my door!"
Quoth the Raven, "Nevermore"

And the Raven, never flitting, still is sitting, still is sitting
On the pallid bust of Pallas just above my chamber door;
And his eyes have all the seeming of a demon's that is dreaming
And the lamp-light o'er him streaming throws his shadows on the floor;
And my soul from out that shadow that lies floating on the floor
Shall be lifted – nevermore!

Edgar Allan Poe

To My Mother

Because I feel that, in the Heavens above,
The angels, whispering to one another,
Can find, among their burning terms of love,
None as devotional as that of "Mother,"
Therefore by that dear name I long have called you –
You who are more than mother unto me,
And fill my heart of hearts, where death installed you
In setting my Virginia's spirit free
My mother – my own mother, who died early,
Was but the mother of myself; but you
Are mother to the one I loved so dearly,
And thus are dearer than the mother I knew
By that infinity with which my wife
Was dearer to my soul than its soul-life

Edgar Allan Poe

Christina Rossetti

(1830- 1894)

Christina Georgina Rossetti was born on December 5, 1830 in London, England and died on December 29, 1894 in London, England also. Christina was the youngest of four siblings. She wrote many poems about fantasy, love and nature, death and religious subject matter. She also wrote children's verses. Christina Rossetti was home schooled. Christina Rossetti was considered one of England's most important women poets in the nineteenth-century.

Remember

Remember me when I am gone away,
Gone far away into the silent land;
When you can no more hold me by the hand,
Nor I half turn to go yet turning stay.
Remember me when no more day by day
You tell me of our future that you planned:
Only remember me; you understand
It will be late to counsel then or pray.
Yet if you should forget me for a while
And afterwards remember, do not grieve:
For if the darkness and corruption leave
A vestige of the thoughts that once I had,
Better by far you should forget and smile
Than that you should remember and be sad

Christina Rossetti

William Shakespeare

(1564-1616)

William Shakespeare was born in late April 1564. His parents were John Shakespeare, father and Mary Arden, mother. There is no record of William Shakespeare's birth. But his baptism was recorded by the church and his birthday is assumed to be the April 23, 1564. Shakespeare was also known as an actor and playwright. He had many friends who were very well connected and influenced many people.

William Shakespeare married Anne Hathaway a few months after she became pregnant. He was in love and had planned to marry another Anne. I guess that by being unfaithful, he stuck to the same first name as to not get confused when speaking to them. The other love was Anne Whateley.

William Shakespeare wrote tragedies such as *Anthony and Cleopatra, Coriolanus, Hamlet, Julius Caesar, King Lear, Macbeth, Othello, Romeo and Juliet,* and *Titus Andronicus.* He also wrote histories of *King Henry IV Part 1, King Henry IV Part 2, King Henry V, King Henry VI Part 1, King Henry VI Part 2, King Henry VI Part 3, King Henry VIII, King John Richard II* and *Richard III.* William Shakespeare wrote comedies such as *All's Well That Ends Well, As You Like It, Comedy of Errors, Cymbeline, Lost, Measure for Measure, Merchant of Venice, Merry Wives of Windsor, Midsummer Night's Dream, Tempest, Troilus and Cressida, Twelfth Night, Two Gentlemen of Verona* and *Winter's Tale.* Shakespeare also wrote an abundance of sonnets, plus other poems including *The Passionate Pilgrim* and *Venus and Adonis.*

To be, or Not to Be

From Hamlet

To be, or not to be – that is the question:
Whether 'tis nobler in the mind to suffer
The slings and arrows of outrageous fortune
Or to take arms against a sea of troubles
And by opposing end them. To die, to sleep
No more – and by a sleep to say we end
The heartache and the thousand natural shocks
That flesh is heir to 'tis a consummation
Devoutly to be wished. To die, to sleep –
To sleep – perchance to dream: ay, there's the rub,
For in that sleep of death what dreams may come
When we have shuffled off this mortal coil,
Must give us pause – There's the respect
That makes calamity of so long life.
For who would bear the whips and scorns of time,
The oppressor's wrong, the proud man's contumely
The pangs of despised love, the law's delay,
The insolence of office, and the spurns
That patient merit of Th' unworthy takes,
When he himself might his quietus make
With a bare bodkin who would fardels bear,
To grunt and sweat under a weary life,
But that the dread of something after death,
The undiscovered country, from whose bourn
No traveler returns, puzzles the will,
And makes us rather bear those ills we have
Than fly to others that we know not of
Thus conscience does make cowards of us all,
And thus the native hue of resolution
Is sicklied o'er with the pale cast of thought,
And enterprise of great pitch and moment
With this regard their currents turn awry
And lose the name of action. – Soft you now,
The fair Ophelia! – Nymph, in thy orisons
Be all my sins remembered

William Shakespeare

Walt Whitman

(1819-1892)

When you think of Whitman... What do you think? Do you think of Whitman's chocolate or Walter Whitman the man, the poet, the great! Walter Whitman was born on May 31, 1819 in Long Island, New York. He was famous for possibly one of the greatest poetry book of all times titled, Leaves of Grass. Walter Whitman adored writing about America, slavery and democracy.

No Labor-Saving Machine

No labor – saving machine,
Nor discovery have I made,
Nor will I be able to leave behind me any wealthy bequest
To found a hospital or library,
Nor reminiscence of any deed of courage for America,
Nor literary success nor intellect, nor book for the book-shelf,
But a few carols vibrating through the air I leave,
For comrades and lovers

Walt Whitman

Beautiful Women

Women sit, or move to and fro – some old, some young;
The young are beautiful – but the old are more beautiful than the young.

Walt Whitman

I Was Looking a Long While

I was looking a long while for a clue
To the history of the past for myself,
And for these chants – and now I have found it;
It is not in those paged fables in the libraries,
Them I neither accept nor reject;
It is no more in the legends than in all else;
It is in the present – it is this earth to-day;
It is in Democracy – the purport and aim of all the past;
It is the life of one man or one woman to-day – the average man of today;
It is in languages, social customs, literatures, arts;
It is in the broad show of artificial things, ships, machinery,
Politics, creeds, modern improvements,
And the interchange of nations,
All for the average man of to-day.

WALT WHITMAN

Present

W. Jude Aher

A Note from the Author

I am a 53 year old male. I was born in Gardner, Massachusetts. I grew up in Opa-Locka, Florida until I was nine years old. Then I lived in New York City (Brooklyn & Queens) until 18. I had a year and half of college at C.C.N.Y. Furthermore I became a poet-artist hippie civil rights activist at 17. Ran amuck hitching about America living my art and street theater upon well into my 30's. Became disabled with progressive Multiple Sclerosis at 41. I never managed my novels due to M.S. Lost my art for seven years but found it again with limits due to M.S. So I live watching a river flow.

Fireflies Dance

on the echo of tears
falling dry
across the ever
African winds
sound dies
from the lips of children
just hopeless sighs
who lie
as dust upon the earth
do you hear
their echoes
dancing across
the rains of silence
falling
falling slow
where
the stains of the child
waiting on death
whose parents eyes
never rest
cry in silence
a silence found
ever
ever more
fireflies dance
across the dusk
long summer days
the 6 o'clock news
tomorrow
maybe tomorrow
because you know
someone,
needs to believe!

W. JUDE AHER

river wind silence

dance me
arms across
seasons
tears,
the water
of my belief

I don't want love
I don't want fear
I just want
the rhythm of your steps
to carry you free

china sea stains
shadow color
across your eyes
clouds try
poets cry

river wind silence
when she
doesn't believe

oh! dance my jester tears,
dance me
arms across seasons.

W. Jude Aher

When She Dances

her Spanish eyes dream
as she sighs
walk the long warm
Mediterranean winds,
they carve her world true.
when she dances
is a woman who believes
in the water mirror
painted across a blue sea,
reflections are the stains
of one who loves deep.
the earth is warm
sifting through her fingers
so sweet those Mediterranean winds,
she carves our world
a deeper hue.

W. Jude Aher

Christopher Aiden

I am a 46 year old American writer who has been living in Chiang Mai, Thailand for the last several years. I was born in Allegheny Co., Pennsylvania. I have been writing sporadic poetry and short stories since I was 12 years old. I had literary pieces published online and in Ancient Heart, Full Moon, and Confused in a Deeper Way magazines. Furthermore, I have poems included in several of the Voicesnet Anthologies. Additionally, along with Siali Tan, an Indonesian writer, my work was published in the Poetically Speaking magazine. Samples of my work can be viewed online at www.poetry-poem.com/chiangmai but a more complete list of titles can be found at www.Internationalpoets.com under user: Aiden is my pen name.

A Place in the Heavens

Where do the stars go
when the clouds get in the
Way?
When rain soaked nights
Fade to dawn and last throughout
the day?
Where do my dreams go
when sleep is gone from my
Eyes?
When darkness moves to
another world and light is reborn
In the skies?
They ride on winds above
The clouds, where the sky
Is always blue,
And search the heavens for the
Stars,
Which keep her dreams
'Till they come true.

Christopher Aiden

Rain Again

For Nitiya

It's hard to see your tears,
when you're crying in the rain.
You can hide them there for years.
No one will see your pain:

I forgot the way she smiled
when I first said; "I love you".
Her ivory skin; so soft and mild,
Is gone like morning dew.

Each day it's easier to forget
some detail important then.
But there's always a time when I just let
her kiss haunt me again.

So now I dream of that kiss,
and remember way back when ...
It's really not a bad day to do this,
It looks like rain again.

Christopher Aiden

Kevin Alawine

Kevin Alawine, author of Thru His Eyes, likes to use his poetry to teach his readers lessons about life. Most of his poems could be defined as "short stories written in poetic form." Kevin seeks to see life, people and situations through the eyes of the Lord Jesus Christ and then writes his stories in an effort to pass those insights along to his readers.

Kevin was born in 1961 in the city of Meridian, Mississippi. He was raised ten miles north of Meridian by his parents, Paul and Margaret Alawine in a small community called Collinsville where he is now a single dad raising two young boys, Caleb (12) and Corey (10) on his own. Though he dreams of someday becoming an occupational writer, Kevin has been employed as a CAD operator and CNC programmer with the same firm for fifteen years.

He is currently working on a children's poetry/story book in his spare time. You can read some of Kevin's work for free or order a copy of his book at www.ThruHisEyes.com.

A Gift for Santa

Very near to the end of each year now
At one end of the Bakersville Mall
There's a big lonely man in a red suit
He's so big and so fat and so tall

And he sits on a throne made of plastic
In a kingdom just thirty feet square
And under his fake beard there's no beard
No reindeer or elves anywhere

Now he's not the same man
from the North Pole
That all of the kids love to see
So I guess you could call him a "fill-in"
But in private he's as mean as can be

His birth name is John Joseph Nelson
But all the old folks call him Joe
And many sad years and bitterness tears
Have caused him to hate people so

So how'd he ever come to be "Santa"?
You wonder (and I wonder too)
All I know for sure is it helps him
To pay for his whiskey and boos

At ten when the mall's doors are closing
Old Joe walks out into the night
He can soon be seen down
at the package liquor store
And from there he soon ducks out of sight

Well, he sleeps in a car in an alley
When the Salvation Army's not his home
And he hits the soup kitchen for breakfast
And the truck stop to bath and to comb

Then he walks up the street passing people
Never waving or speaking at all
And he curses the shoppers there
under his breath
As he makes his way up to the mall

And he dreads every child he will see there
And he hates them behind his fake smile
But for the sake of his boos and his whiskey
He can stand it at least for a while

One day as he sits in his tall chair
He reflects on the past he hates so
In his mind he slips back
through the sad years
To the man that he was long ago

He remembers how he was a father
And a husband so truly in love
And how he would teach Joey Junior
To worship the Lord up above

He remembers his lovely young Julie
A beautiful lady indeed
And how they would tuck little Joey
In his bed and the Bible they'd read

And how they would pray there with Joey
That Jesus would watch over him
For angels to stand guard around him
And protect him through thick and through thin

"Oh dear God! How I hate to remember!
That's my reason for drinking you see
As I walk in this curse, I my bitterness nurse
And my enemy is my memory!"

He remembers that night on the freeway
He remembers the screeching of tires
He remembers the cries and the screaming
He remembers the gasoline fire

He remembers the ambulance siren
He remembers the hospital bed
He remembers the sound of the doctor's sad voice
Saying, "Sorry, your baby is dead"

He remembers the following Sunday
He remembers the sermon on sin
He remembers walking out of the church house
Saying, "I'll never be back here again"

He remembers the day that his Julie left home
He remembers the fight that they had
He remembers how he yelled, "Good riddance!"
Too numb to even feel sad

And as he sits there and remembers
He is lost in a long silent pause
He is finally brought back to the present
As a little voice says, "Mr. Claus?"

And there on the floor at his feet now
Is the cutest boy he's ever seen
The big dark brown eyes are quite a surprise
Beside that tall tree, Christmas green

"Hi, Mr. Santa! I'm Tommy!"
He hears a little squeaky voice say
"And I've come to sit in your lap now
But I have a short list here today"

And Joe thinks, "Indeed, yes, a short list
Ha! Right! Now what a thing to say!
I've never seen a brat with a short list
and I sit here every single day!"

And Tommy climbs up in his lap then

And pulls out a paper so small
Joe thinks, "That's the least list
that I've seen
In all of my years in this mall"

Then Tommy looks up at old "Santa"
His big pretty eyes seem to shine
"My dad lost his job at the factory
But I told my mom that it's fine"

"I would like a B.B. gun, Santa
But if that's too much, it's okay
I didn't come to ask you for anything
No, I have got something to say"

"You see, about two or three weeks ago
While I was at church with my mom
The pastor had just preached a sermon
And then asked the Spirit to come"

"And while Mrs. Jones played piano
I felt a sharp pain deep within
And I knew in my heart it was Jesus
Wanting to cleanse me from sin"

"I cried as I walked to the alter
The pastor then taught me a prayer
I asked God to wash and to cleanse me
And He came in my heart standing there"

"And right there the weight of sin left me
I knew I was free as could be
I wanted to pay back the Savior
For paying the penalty for me"

"And on my way home I was praying
For Jesus to show me the way
That I could do something to pay back
For how He had saved me that day"

And I thought, "Hey, my Sunday School teacher
Has told us before many times
We help God by just helping others
The weak and the sick and the blind"

"And wanting to be sure I helped out
The one He would want me to help
I prayed and I prayed and I asked Him
Determined to do this myself"

"I prayed and I prayed through the nighttime
And then fell asleep just because
I hadn't had sleep and sir I then dreamed
Of praying for you, Santa Claus"

"So today sir, I come with no money
I come with no ribbons or bows
I don't have a dime; I've only my time
But the greatest of gifts, I suppose"

"Cause Jesus has told me to pray sir
And no matter the trouble or pain
When Jesus says pray, we should start right away
'Cause Jesus says nothing in vain"

"And sir, I admit I am humbled
To pray for someone such as you
But I feel that the good Lord has told me
That even St. Nick can be blue"

"Maybe your reindeers are sickly
Maybe your wife has the flu
Maybe your elves have been hurting themselves
Working so hard like they do"

"I don't really know Mr. Santa
Exactly what your problem is
But I know that there isn't a problem
That Jesus can't take on as His"

Old Joe, he can't speak for a moment
And besides, he doesn't know what to say
But finally he manages to choke up
Just one little word he says, "Pray"

And Tommy says, "Oh what a privilege!
To pray for a man such as you!
I'm so very nervous Mr. Santa
I don't really know what to do"

He then lays his hands on old Joe there
And he prays him a short little prayer
He takes Joe's rough old hands in his hands
And asks God to bless him right there

"Our Father in heaven, I ask You
To please bless poor Santa today
Please watch him and keep him and bless him
And don't let fear get in his way"

"And Jesus I forgot to tell him
The most precious part of my dream
As beautiful as it was to me
It didn't make sense so it seemed"

"I saw a little boy up in heaven
He was singing oh so beautifully
He waved and said, "Please tell my Daddy
I've got angels standing all around me!"

"Well, I didn't know this boy's daddy
But I figured if anyone did
That it would be Santa for certain
He knows every mom, dad and kid"

"Well, My mom will be wanting me home soon
So I have to go pretty quick
I thank You my Father for letting me give
This present to good old St. Nick"

With that Tommy drops to the mall floor
And he soon runs away out of sight
And something is different about old Joe
When they lock up the mall doors that night

He makes his way right past the liquor store
Without even slowing his pace
He goes to his old car in the alley
And spends the whole night on his face

He cries and he cries out to God now
He cries and he cries then some more
And he asks the Lord Jesus to take out of him
The bitterness that's made him so sore

And he asks the Lord God to forgive him
And to touch him afresh and anew
He says, "Lord, I'm waiting for You now!"
But God says, "I've been waiting for you"

Joe's life changes swiftly in the following days
Through his eyes there's a whole different view
And soon he is offered a very good job
Of doing what he used to do

And old Joe now works as a teller
At the Bakersville National Bank
And he has the Lord God and the Spirit
And cute little Tommy to thank

But he made the bank sign an agreement
A contract that they are sworn to
To let Joe have free time near Christmas
'Cause he has a job he must do

And very near to the end of each year now
At one end of the Bakersville Mall
There's a big jolly man in a red suit
He's so happy, so fat and so tall

And he sits on a throne made of plastic
In a kingdom just thirty feet square
And under his fake beard there's no beard
But there's always a smile under there

Now he's not the same man from the North Pole
That all of the kids love so much
So I guess you could call him a "fill-in"
But he now has the Spirit's sweet touch

I don't think that even the "real" Claus
With his reindeer and magic and snow
Could have such a great love for people
As our precious old Bakersville Joe

'Cause Joe finally asked God to fill him
With the Spirit that comes down from above
But he had to let go of his bitterness
So that Jesus could fill him with love

Kevin Paul Alawine

Happy Mother's Day

When I think back as far as I can remember
You were always there for me
The security I felt in your presence
As I followed around at your feet

The sweet smell of food in the kitchen
The faded old apron you wore
The kisses that said, "Boy, I love you!"
There was nothing that I needed more

I cannot remember, not one single thing
That I ever set out to do
That you didn't help to encourage
I could just do it, you knew

When I was no longer your baby
You watched me grow taller each day
And you watched me get awfully rebellious
But you hung in there with me anyway

We went through the stage when I "knew everything"
Yet I didn't want to get out of bed
When I think of the mouth that I had on me then
I don't know why you didn't knock off my head

Yes, my generation was going to change the world
By partying all night I suppose
And though it doesn't make sense to me now
Well, that was the life that I chose

When I think of late nights that you wondered where I was
Or if I was even alive
I knew in my heart you weren't sleeping
Until you had heard me arrive

You taught me all about heaven
Though I dragged your poor heart straight through hell
I know that you wondered if I would ever repent
Or I'd die or I'd wind up in jail

Praise the Lord! For He brought me right out of that life
Though my flesh tried so hard to resist
And I know that you were my personal prayer warrior
And my very first evangelist

Mothers are so often taken for granted
Though they storm the gates of hell in their love
Like Christ they have to lay down their very lives
With a passion that comes down from above

If I spent all the time from now 'till I die
There's no way I could ever repay
Hopefully I can find some things I can do
To make your life better someday

You've taught me by example
That's the way you've lived your life
And you've taught me what a mother is
A lady and a wife

Mama, for some time now it's bothered me that I've written a poem for Daddy and one for each of the boys. I've written Pam's testimony and dedicated a poem to her but as of yet I haven't written anything for you. I've been waiting for the right inspiration and the right words. When I've tried to write for you nothing was ever good enough. I hope this will do.
Mama I love you,
Love, Kevin

KEVIN PAUL ALAWINE

Elein Arencibia

Elein Arencibia was born in March 22nd, 1983 in Miami, Florida. Raised in a very talkative Cuban household, she is known for quickly saying what's on her mind. She would always see her father write poetry to express his love for her and her mom. When Elein reached middle school, she began to be interested in writing poetry. During high school, her interest kicked into high gear and she began writing poetry whenever she felt inspired; despite what time it was or where she was. Elein is now a senior at Florida International University and will graduate with a B.S. in Elementary Education with ESOL Endorsement on December 2005.

Encounters

Endings, beginnings,
Nows, yesterdays, tomorrows. They
can't be forgotten or
overseen. In this world there are
Us', I's, you's and they's. But,
never forget they all equal
to one thing: we're all brothers in this
Endless
Rollercoaster we like to call life.
So, never forget to smile to your fellow brothers.

ELEIN ARENCIBIA

Reality?

Unpolished ways
Crazy thoughts
Can you really tell what's real?

What ever happened
to choosing your path?
Knowing your destiny

Now you sit
Wondering if.
Can you really know?

Know tomorrow.
What you'll do.
What you'll say.
Who you'll meet

you know your type and
Fantasies boggle your mind.
You meet Mr. No-so-Perfect.

But he's exactly what you want.
So now you wonder:
Can you really tell what's real?

Elein Arencibia

Marcy Axness, Ph.D.

Marcy Axness, Ph.D. is an award-winning documentary writer/producer in her "pre-motherhood" life; Marcy Axness turned her penetrating eye to early human development when her own children were born (18 and 14 years ago.) Using as a narrative foundation her experiences as an adoptee and a mother, Dr. Axness researches, teaches and writes about attachment, adoption, pregnancy, parenting and... *Life!*

Dr. Axness is a regular columnist for a Los Angeles parenting publication, and over the past dozen years has had short pieces in *Time, Harper's Bazaar, USA Today,* and the *Los Angeles Times Sunday Magazine,* and feature articles in *The Whole Life Times, L.A. Family,* and *Roots & Wings Adoption Magazine.* She has also published several scholarly articles in peer-reviewed journals in such disparate fields as theology and prenatal psychology, and her articles have appeared in a variety of adoption training manuals internationally.

Mainly a non-fiction writer, Dr. Axness admits that "Once Removed" is the closest thing to a poem she has published. The second closest thing (but as yet unpublished) is her "fictional memoir" novel *Upon Waking,* which was the unconventional centerpiece of her doctoral dissertation; it has been widely praised by scholarly as well as popular readers. Dr. Axness is on the faculty of Santa Barbara Graduate Institute and has a private counseling and education practice in Los Angeles, specializing in fertility, pregnancy psychology, adoption and early parenting. Weaving together scientific and spiritual principles, with a focus on clients' narratives, her *Quantum Parenting* approach offers parents avenues for discovering how to support their child's healthiest development from pre-conception/pre-adoption, while unfolding their own parenting magnificence. You are invited to read more of her articles or contact Dr. Axness at her website, www.QuantumParenting.com.

[This autobiographical essay appears as a prelude in Jane Guttman's powerful book, *The Gift Wrapped in Sorrow,* in which she chronicles the pain, surrender, and healing she has experienced as a birthmother. In her introduction to the following, Jane wrote, "In the course of writing this book I have become intimately related to the pain of adoption. But I can only truly know *my* pain. It has been of the utmost importance to me to also become aware of what it feels like to be surrendered. I believe it is essential to include an impression of that experience as well."]

Once Removed

Once removed.

That is how I have felt for most of my life. Standing apart *once removed* from the stuff of real, human life. Outside *once removed* looking in, an alien. Exempt from some invisible, inscrutable core human experience *connection* that seemed to initiate everyone else into some grand cosmic family to which I was merely a step-child. An adopted child. A surrendered child.

Cast in the fire of disconnection. Unplanned. A mistake. An inconvenience. Carried by a mother who saw me as a "gift" she was making for a nice, infertile couple. My first mother didn't so much reject me as much as simply fail to claim me as a significant part of her own life, even during her pregnancy. I suffered from premature relinquishment, since she let me go *once removed* without ever really having me.

All of my relationships found their blueprint in that foundational indifference, and shaped themselves around the invisible *once removed* scars on my soul. My adulthood became a stage whereupon I reenacted that first intimate relationship, in which I felt too loosely held, too faintly regarded, too unclaimed. So I would urge my co-star of the moment *claim me for the moment find me good find me fine find me so I can find me too.* And they would, for awhile. But a force no less than Destiny herself had deemed me *once removed* unkeepable. My co-stars always fulfilled the obligations of their role, to not be able to give me what I needed, to agree to part amicably, *indifferently,* to set up the inevitable scene for me: *I find my way back to the void.*

I have found healing by stepping into that void, by staring down into the endless black of it. My gift in return for that harrowing journey is a life with connection, with a loving husband, a beautiful family. But the knowledge is still there. The truth is still there. Down there deep, where the snake resides, where my body resists going, fighting it with every fiber, every cell, fighting by simply stepping down to an idle so slow that I might simply stall out. Yes, the truth is still there, coiled up and waiting: the primary, shaping reality of my life, *disconnection.* It is where I still revert in times of stress or trauma, because that is how my brain and my psyche are wired. I was cast in the fire of separation, and despite all my years of tender and compassionate tending of that wound, despite all the years of carefully constructing a life that includes intimate connections, my body knows that at the core of me still squalls that *once removed* baby in the void... insignificant... alone.

And yet, just as true is that the years unspool, and Destiny reveals a sliver of the Big Picture at a time... We reunite. We struggle, we ache, we thrill, we drink in echoes of our selves reflected in the other. We dabble in the folly of trying to recoup the lost years. We reenact the severed connection in our poignant and feeble human attempt to create a different outcome, to somehow make it right. But it cannot be made right. It just is. And when we can hold that brutal truth, we are no longer *once removed* disconnected, from each other, from ourselves, from humanity, from God.

MARCY WINEMAN AXNESS, PH.D.

Nathaniel Booker

A Note from the Poet, Nathaniel Booker from Baltimore, Maryland, United States of America

I am a 34 year old African-American male. I am a divorced father of 2, one boy and one girl; I am also engaged. I have been writing since I was eleven years old. I write about hurt and pain and the very essence of life and beauty as I see it. I am an aspiring writer and each step I take on the road of life brings me closer to that goal.

I have been writing since I was eleven years old as it became a way of expressing the overwhelming pain that I endured in my childhood and young adulthood. I have since learned to accept and come to terms with my past and I strive to use it as a way to help those who are also troubled with life.

Can I?

Can I be the lock that fits your key?
Can I be the light that helps you see?
On cold winter nights can I be the heat,
That removes the chill and warms your feet;
and can I be the truth that sets you free?

Can I be the moon and you my earth?
If I were a diamond, would you be my worth?
Can I be the house that you make your home?
Can I be the reason you're never alone?

If you were a princess and found yourself sold,
could I be the elf who spins your gold?
If you were locked high up in a castle steep,
could I be the knight who rescues you from the dragons keep?

Can I be your warm blanket when the nights are cold?
Can I spend my life with you as you grow old?
When the sky is clear and the sun is high,
can I speak to you as you pass by?

When it's time to leave and you're on your way,
can I be the reason that makes you stay?
When you're tired and worn and the day has been long,
can I be your hot bath and your sweet soothing song?

Can I be your hero and your daunting black knight?
Can I share dinner with you by candle light?
Can I be the one kissing you when our lips draw near,
and can I be the one showing you, there's nothing to fear?

Can I bring you red roses with baby's breath,
and thirst quenching water when there is none left?
Can I tell you my dream where we are together,
and that if it ever came true, I'd love you forever?

What I'm saying is that you'd be my reason for living,
and even if you reject me, I'll never stop giving.
Some questions need asking, so I ask you, Can I?
Can I love you and live for you until the day that I die?

NATHANIEL A. BOOKER, SR
"Genius Under Construction"

The Last Petal

A single long stemmed rose I'd given to you,
symbolizes the love that we share.
Its petals are red, it's next to our bed
and its scent perfectly fills the air.

It bloomed the day we first fell in love,
and has continued to bloom ever since;
A vision of perfection, it mirrors our affection,
how it hurts to recall these events.

We began to argue over trivial things,
and never noticed that a rose petal fell.
Its descent was long and it hit like a bomb,
with its impact, love's end it did spell.

Everything used to be in sync for us,
our goings, our comings and such.
But now petals are scattered, our love's all but shattered,
how I long to touch you so much.

It's hard to imagine we'd be where we are,
when our love started off so strong.
But like the petals on this rose, so our love goes,
if we don't grasp it, it soon will be gone.

A love like ours is so hard to acquire,
but like snow in the sun, it dissolves.
So, with our loving embrace, the bad times, let's erase,
before the last rose petal falls.

NATHANIEL BOOKER
"Genius Under Construction"

Winter in My Heart

She gave me her love
but I couldn't accept it;
thought she'd take it away
and I would sorely regret it.

She kissed me gently,
and I turned away;
she asked how I felt,
I had nothing to say.

She reached for me
and I withdrew;
She said, I only want
to be with you.

I looked at her gently,
then I closed my eyes;
same response as always,
she wasn't surprised.

How can I tell her
I don't know how to feel;
I have love in my heart
but I'm not sure that it's real.

Spring turns to summer,
then autumn plays its part,
but no matter what I do or what I say,
it's always winter in my heart.

She brought home some passion
to rekindle my fire,
but other than the physical pleasure
I had no desire.

No desire for love
I didn't want to hold hands,
I wouldn't look to the future
she was not in my plans.

I couldn't trust her to love her,
although she loved me completely,
she thought that if she loved me
that her love would defeat me.

I looked at her solemnly
and to her I said,
all of the words
that often swirl in my head.

My beautiful friend,
I cannot give what I do not possess,
I do not know love,
for me, betrayal is best.

I am the Ice Prince,
I am devoid of emotion,
my kisses spell death
to the likes of love and devotion.

I have an old soul;
it's both my blessing and curse,
so the love that you feel for me
can never come first.

I care for you deeply,
I swear that I do,
I could tell you that I love you
but it wouldn't be true.

You are better of catching dreams
in the palm of your hand,
because the freezing depths of my heart,
you can never withstand.

I could take all of your love,
and I could be with you only,
but at the end your lifeline,
you'd be broken and lonely.

She looked at me softly
with tender tears in her eyes;
she ran from me, fled from me,
I wasn't surprised.

Several weeks later
when after work I came home,
all of her belongings were gone,
and I was there all alone.

A note in the bathroom
was all that remained;
her shade of lipstick on the mirror
is where she wrote out her shame.

To my dearly beloved,
it's with great pain that I write this,
but if my guess is correct,
my presence you do not miss.

I gave all I had,
I gave you all that I could,
I gave you more love
than any one person should.

I know the depths of your pain,
and what fuels your deep inner sorrow,
I wanted to bear it,
I wanted to be your tomorrow.

But you just wouldn't let me;
you were so self-absorbed;
I got nothing in return
for all of the love that I poured.

I know that you wanted
a bitter goodbye,
you wanted me to be angry
and with no tears in my eyes.

But I won't renege on the love
that I promised to you;
I might be saying good-bye
but I'm sad and I'm blue.

No words can describe,
and no emotion can measure,
the love that I have for you,
you're really missing a treasure.

I pray you come around
and that you soon clear your head,
come claim the love that's yours
when the Ice Prince is dead.

The love in my heart
it can't wait forever,
I can't promise I'll be here,
so we might not be together.

Believe that I love you
it hurts so much to depart,
and that all the love I have for you
can't overcome the winter in your heart.

I closed my eyes and I felt
an indescribable feeling,
somewhere deep in my heart,
the ice was revealing,

An inner warmth and a feeling
of deeply rooted emotion,
a need to be loved
and a desire for devotion.

The woman I love,
I let slip away;
My reflection looks accusingly,
I have nothing to say.

The Ice Prince is dead,
I can feel it, he's gone,
but look how I've aged,
he's been gone for so long.

I rushed from the house,
I headed to the Church for Confession,
but I can't get inside
because of the Wedding Procession,

So I slip into the Church,
I sit in the very last pew,
I glimpse the Bride as she passes,
and to my horror, its you.

You look into my row
and our eyes lock with a start,
and in a flash every scene plays
that was buried deep in my heart.

I find myself reaching,
but I failed and I faltered,
when I look up there you are,
standing before the altar.

If these two shouldn't marry,
I ask that you speak now,
the Holy Father beseeched,
and I just held my head down.

I wanted you, I needed you,
but I couldn't deny,
another man who appreciated,
what I failed to see in your eyes.

Your wedding vows were said
and your devotions exchanged,
it's not me that you're marrying,
and it suddenly feels strange.

All eyes are upon me
as I'm standing here crying,
the final block of ice chipped away
and I feel like I'm dying.

I stand outside of the Church
with all of the rice throwers
and I watch as you pass
and you toss away your flowers.

You walk up to me
before you float out of my life,
and I can't help but be jealous and covet,
another man's wife.

I can see that you are sad,
and I know you've been crying,
but you are a beautiful man,
there is no denying.

You are hurting right now,
I am not going to gloat,
it hurts you'll be sailing
alone in that boat.

But I know someday if you let it,
your heart will find love,
and all the joy you deserve
that you've never dreamt of.

And I for my part,
deep in my heart I will miss you,
I'll cry tears of joy and
dab my eyes with a tissue.

Finally she said
as she turned to depart,
So this is what it took
to melt the ice within you heart.

I watched her as she rode away
to the life I refused to give her
I thought I would be bitter,
but I only longed to be there with her.

A tear rolled down my cheek,
and dried in the Summer air;
No more crying, no more dying,
now my heart has love to share.

Now I know the seasons change,
summer and spring and then autumn plays its part,
but I vow to look for love and hold on to it,
there's no more winter in my heart.

NATHANIEL BOOKER
"Genius Under Construction"

Janelle-Diane Bravo

Janelle Bravo celebrates her birthday every year on August 23rd with family and friends. She is a very prim and proper young lady who enjoys living and laughing. Janelle is keen on spending time with loved ones. She is currently a student at Florida International University.

Mom

The other day I looked at my hands
They looked to me like yours
It wasn't the color
Or the little freckles I found
It was something else.

It was the habits you have shown me
The unconditional love you have given me
The nurturing skills you have passed down
The wisdom you have instilled in me
The reassurance you have offered me.

But most of all, dearest mother,
The other day I looked at my hands
They looked to me like yours
It wasn't the color
Or the little freckles I found
It was the never-ending hope to someday be
The mother you have been to us.

Janelle-Diane Bravo

Isabel Cabán

A Note from the Author

Let me begin by announcing myself as one of the most fortunate women on this earth. I am 37 years young with an amazing family and a bright perspective on this bitter-sweet existence that this world has blessed us with. I am Cuban-American and reside in Miami, Florida with my husband, Sean and two children; Romani, age 12, and Mia Juliet, age 7. We are healthy and active parents who enjoy travel in our RV, boating, and playing racquetball and bowling with our kids. Romi and Mia both enjoy the ocean water and like to play basketball, board games and swim in our pool everyday that God makes that sun possible.

Romani and Mia represent the glory and true purpose of my life. Along the way of this miraculous path of being their mother, I tend to my career as a personal trainer and to the various responsibilities of being a wife, a daughter, a sister and a niece to my beloved family. My children and spouse are my inspiration for writing poetry and as I read it to them, I bring them into a world that is just us, and eventually will include you, the reader of my world. One way of giving something back to society is to share my feelings with you. Maybe you have felt what I have felt, or are feeling it now. Regardless, here it is, in black and white and as bright as day to make you feel something that may be or that someday may become. Thank you.

Being Your Wife

The wind chime on my window top is you
The sounds of love go through me
As I wallow in your noise
Rejoice in bliss, fulfill my kiss
And never mind life's needed poise
I want to dance along your wind
And follow your parade in song
Your children rest under your wing
Then laughing, frolic in the sun
I'll polish up my wedding ring
Now more than ever we are strong
For finally we have prevailed
And truth now binds our vows
Our offspring draws us from the frowns
And hold us closely in their hearts
Open your eyes to much surprise
We are each other's wind chime
Open your soul and see the glory in your life
You have it all right here and now
So harmonize and smile upon your rise
I am quite proud to be your wife…

My Dearest Love, Sean
Happy Father's Day

Isabel Cabán

Our Precious Little One

Hello, you there inside of me
The precious little you is much too grand
Can you feel my hand?
I'll warm you further when I bathe
Than your surrounding seas
And you will dine the finest treats that grow from greens and trees
The earth has raised fine fruit and I will pass it on, to make you strong
I won't indulge, no time for wine,
I wouldn't want to do you wrong
I will not fib, for plans did not include a crib
But you are here and surely so
The only innocence I know
I'll raise you lovingly with honor
We'll be alright; we'll have our cake and bake our pie
You'll have the roots we will provide
Someday your wings will let you fly
We cannot yield your very fear, for at times pain will educate and suffering will teach you
The know-how of the streets, a must
As well as orchestra, Van Gogh,
Shakespeare or bust
If I shall pass before the wheel and cruise
Promise your goals you will not loose
Diplomas shine upon your wall
Your dignity upheld and just
Follow your dreams, go for it all
Remember Romi, it is you that I adore
You're everything I need and more
Have fun, enjoy and savoir life
Make sure your best friend is your wife
Be happy Darling, stay safe and sweet
Our souls will someday come to meet
Live for the moment, one then another
And take this with you always…
…You are my life,
Love, Your Mother

Isabel Cabán

The Wish

What is a wish? Do they come true?
How can we beat the odds
Things never happen the way we plan
Just let it go and let things fly the way they can

Isn't that the way to change the world
Think of the bad so that it will not happen
Wish for the things you do not want
Why that is, no one knows
And we can't beat the way it goes

When I need you I'll wish you far away
Then surprisingly so, you'll be right there as bright as day

When I need peace I'll wish for war
And there will be not one new scar
For soon enough I'll breathe fresh air without a care

When I want love I'll reach for fear
And right away goodness appears
So many ways to count your blessings
But think how many you desired and reached
The ones that came were not your own
Your birthday wish – another's lips that candle blown

I promise that the only truth in life is not to hurry
Take your time to laugh and play and sing in days of showers
For all that comes shall anyway no matter days or hours

Isabel Cabán

Didier Camacho

A Note from the Author

I am a 25-year-old Cuban-American, majoring in Geology at Florida International University. I will be graduating in July 2006. I am also a Christian, who has faith in God and gives thanks to the beautiful sights this world has to offer. I am a writer who is inspired by moments, sights and sounds. Poetry is not whether it is good or bad, or if it rhymes or not, it's about the author's story. But, to others who read it, it is a place of escape, fantasy, illusion, tears or reality. That's what special about poetry: the poet writes with one specific meaning in mind, but the reader decides where to take it.

Innocent Awakening

In the morning when you wake
Smile; so the sun can brighten up your day.

In the morning when you rise
Smile; so you can bring joy into a poor child's eyes.

In the morning when there's rain;
Smile; gently caressing a dying man's pain.

In the morning if it's melancholy;
Smile; and the swans will play their melody.
In the morning when you look toward the mountains;
Smile; imagining at the top are your sapphire fountains.

Brighten a life,
Brighten a soul,
but it's the candor in your smile
that makes you glow. . .

Didier Camacho

Turning Tides

Stranger by the shore away in dreams of doves' peace
Nature's symphony has inspired gentle belle,
for alas be still kind heart.
Madding tis' the storm that makes him faint.
Has kindred princess galloped away in Arabian towards enchanting renaissance?
The soul sings weary as anchors shackle his spirit.
Walk gentle into the sole, as peace in dreams will come.
While the cool meadows breeze washes away with the tides.

DIDIER CAMACHO

Richard Caruso

Richard Caruso was born, raised, and lived most of my life in Peoria, Illinois, until October, 2001. Whereupon he moved to Safford, Arizona, for the shorter winters.

What Richard likes most about being a substitute teacher is watching the learners' eyebrows raised in delight that freshly open door that was never opened before, that pleasing apparent but humble smile that a student shows with just a little bit of direction. It is not obvious everyday but when it does it as refreshing as morning dew to all of instructor's senses. Also as a substitute it is almost impossible to get into a rut because of the constantly rotating classes one has to cover.

Interview with Richard Caruso

What is your date of birth? Do you have brothers and/or sisters?

Born November 4, 1951, at a weight of almost 11lbs.

The nurses thought I was to be twins.

One other brother, 4 years older, Melvin Caruso.; A computer specialist living in Battle Creek, Michigan

When did you start writing and what inspired you to start?

Early elementary school; a school in Peoria,

Illinois, once called Reservoir Grade School, now named Washington Grade School. In Reservoir Grade School, I believe it was 3rd grade, a teacher very early in the morning was talking about literature and asked, "This question is for all 35 of you, How would you explain the beginning of this day?" We were rather young for such a rather complex question, and the teacher knew it. The class became quiet quickly; every third grade student was waiting for someone else to answer her. I looked around and saw the stumped look on the 34 others. I looked into the teacher's eyes and said, "The breaking of dawn." She smiled and said, "That's very poetic, especially at this age." She went on to prove that she was sincere in her compliment by even repeating it, she said, "Did everybody here that?" The breaking of dawn," she said out loud.

Other than writing, what else do you enjoy doing?

Tending to my subtropical plants that are somewhat difficult to grow at this 3,200 foot elevation; like small date tree sprouts and tangerine sprouts.

Following world news events on television, radio, and the internet; Surfing the internet, occasionally.

Going into the very nearby mountains Of Mt. Graham, to play in the snow, then coming back down to 60 degree January average noon high of Safford, with its palm lined main boulevard. Also the nearby mountains put on an occasional show of low scooting clouds hovering in and out of the mountains valleys. A very soothing site to watch that performs mostly in the cooler months of the year.

What are the titles of your books?

Carusoism & Carusoism II

Do you have a Web site? What is the URL address?

My website is currently entitled, Carusoism and the Cradle of Souls. **www.carusoism.com**

What do you hope to achieve in the future?

Like most people to hopefully stay healthy. Also to maybe travel again, especially after retirement of only about 9 years from now, and its hard to say what else might be of interest to me in the coming future.

RICHARD CARUSO,
Emergency Substitute Teacher, Stone Sculptor, Poet

A Poet

I want to be a poet
To write lines every day
And look in the morning mirror
To watch every hair turn grey
I want to be a poet
To observe the good
As well as the unkind
To prove I am not blind
I want to be a poet
Not because of any pay
But because I must say
What I feel every day
I want to be a poet
With words as a friend
To easily come across
While in your room or den

Richard Caruso

Nature Plays

I rest deep within this scene
Of waves that talk and beach serene
To every life dreams must cling
But here I love of natural things
The silver glitter of oceans' glaze
Among the fish where otters play
The whistling winds that tickle waves
Bring shiny blinks to sunny days
The waves that meet the beaches edge
Seem to drive an emotional edge
Back to the womb with water all around
A feeling so soft and quiet of sound
A smell of moisture fills the air
With a breeze it comes to cool my hair
My feelings rise with every new wave
To every whim that nature plays

Richard Caruso

Winter Night Moon Tree

Blacker than black
This naked tree
Full moon beaming
Behind this leafless tree

The dark and dreary
Has a beauty I know
That is only more eerie
With a full moon's glow

With black winding branches
Piercing a cold starry sky
It almost seems alive
With moon beams that slide

Its deep black beauty
Mixed with a silent scene
Oh full moon of silver
Is its only quiver so clean

RICHARD CARUSO

Todd Cheney

Todd Cheney was born in Brookfield, Wisconsin on a stormy Tuesday morning in 1978. He spent most of his childhood in and around Brookfield, a suburb of Milwaukee. His father was an elevator engineer, but is now retired. His mother is a social worker. His parents divorced in 1987, when he was nine years old. He has moved around the eastern Wisconsin area since then, but has never lived in a different state. The second child of four, Todd has two brothers, one older and one younger, and a younger sister.

Eulogy to Scary Bug

We're here today
to remember the life
of Scary Bug. He was
a good friend, an
excellent father to
three million other
bugs and a true
person in every
sense of the word.
I remember going
out on the town
with him. He used
to regale us with
stories of all his
hapless victims while
holding a beer in
forty-six of his
arms.

Scary Bug
liked to scare
people and that's how
I think he wants to
be remembered.
Back in the nest, when
we were just hatchling
bugs a couple weeks ago,
I asked him what he
wanted to do
with his life.
"Scare people
in the shower," he said.
Yes, Scary Bug,
you certainly did.

I recall now
the day that Scary Bug
Ate the Big One.
He was just minding
his own business in the
shower of a young man's
house.

But the young man
(who happens to think
he's a writer for some
psychotic reason) in the
shower at the time
freaked out and
splashed around at our
friend Scary
hoping he would scurry
away on his many
legs.
The young man hoped he
could wash our friend
down the drain.
But Scary clung
tenaciously to the
shower wall.
Alas, the young man
picked up a shampoo
bottle and struck
Scary with it
splitting his body in
twain.

But he had not finished
yet.
The young man proceeded
to smack the heck out of
Scary, until he was little
more than a pile of tangled
legs and gross mucus
splattered against
the plastic shower
wall.

I should know (begins
to choke up) I was there,
watching from the
ceiling.

I ask that we all now
bow our heads in
a moment of silence
for the dearly
departed.
And now...

The Hymn!

Oh! Scary Bug!
Your many legs
are twirling
in the young man's
shower
you've scared your
last today

Oh! Fearful day!
The shampoo
bottle's deadly smacking!
Your life away
now you reside in
Bug Heaven

and Scary Bug!
We will all
miss you (except for the young
man!) We will
all remember
the light and truth
of all your life.

Now you reside in
Bug Heaven
Now he's gone
away.

Todd Cheney

God's In

Here all around
nowhere else
it's in the smallest
Particle
The faintest
Hope
That
I see my circumspect life
Reflected
in divinity

Todd Cheney

To Arms

Oh! Take up the pen
Young man
Young woman
For before it empires tremble
Leaders fall
Wills are changed

Take up the word
Of what you feel is
True
Take up the banner
For around you the
Walls crumble
Their integrity compromised

Words march forth
Each a soldier in the army of
Language
Each with his sword
His armor
His shield
The meaning cuts
Yet the lines of the letters
Protect

The army is the mind
And only through the mind
Can a battle be won

Oh! Take up the word!

TODD CHENEY

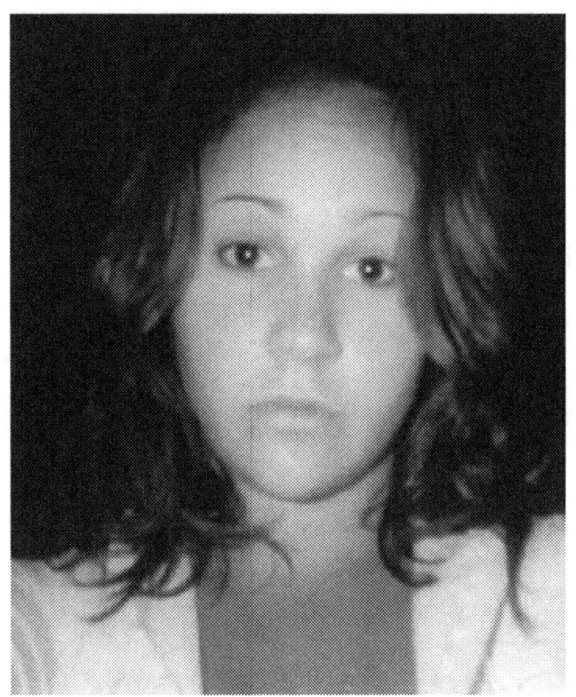

Tahlia Dago

A Note from the Author

I, Tahlia was born on August 28, 1985 in South Miami Hospital. I'm a Virgo! My major is in communications. My future goal is to move out on my own by next year to finish college and figure out what I want to do with my life. The places I have considered are New York, California or New Orleans. The experience will help me grow a lot. This will allow me the opportunity to "find myself" creatively, as an individual. This is something I've always wanted to do and I finally feel ready to do it.

Me

When I look in the mirror,
I see the face
Of a unique girl
Which blonde hair and blue eyes can't replace.
I see a Cuban-American Princess
Whose dark Spanish eyes and brown hair
Set her apart from all the rest.
(She even gets a dimple when her nostrils flare!)

When I look in the mirror,
There is a pair of Gucci's stating something to be told:
This is a reflection
That breaks the average mold –
She is an exception,
She has her own style.

When I look in the mirror,
I see a beauty mark at the corner of her smile.
It's a face made perfect due to imperfections scattered like stars:
Two birthmarks framing the right eye,
On the left of her nose is a tiny scar,
And on that very side, on her cheekbone
Her trademark mole lies alone.

Most importantly,
It all adds up to ME:
Someone I'm proud to be,
When I look into the mirror

Tahlia Dago

Adriana Gale

Adriana Gale is an elementary school teacher in Miami, Florida. She graduated from Florida International University with a Bachelor's Degree in Specific Learning Disabilities, as well as, a Master's Degree in Reading Education. She comes from a very diverse background. Adriana was born in Guayaquil, Ecuador and raised in Caracas, Venezuela, with Spanish and Colombian parents. Adriana loves teaching, reading, watching movies, and relaxing at the beach with a good book. She currently lives in Homestead, Florida with her husband John, dog Toby and Cockatiels Petey and Sophie.

When We First Met

It was love at first sight. His big brown eyes reflected joy as well as sadness. His hair was fine and silky. When I caressed his face, I felt as if I were touching the clouds. His body was slim and dark. I was touched by his tenderness, and fascinated by his outgoing personality. I had never met anyone like him.

When it was time to go, the fear of not seeing him again took over me. We left, and it was almost impossible to stop thinking about him. I couldn't get him of my mind. "We have to go back!" I begged my husband, so we went back to the puppy store and bought him.

ADRIANA GALE

Stacy Goll

A Note from the Author

I started writing when I was around 10 or so, give or take a year or two. Can't remember what started it, but I do know that my father had a strong influence that lit the spark which got me writing. I've always been interested in writing, reading, and art because of my father and mother, and because I like to know about things and expression of personal matters and otherwise. Writing has been a major part of my life ever since I started and it has had a great impact not only for me personally, but many who have seen my works. I'm glad I could bring such enjoyment and inspiration to those who seek it. Granted, most of my work may be dark and emotional, but it brings out the most feeling and expression. I hope you enjoy it as much as I enjoyed creating and composing it.

http://www.geocities.com/catwulf/

I also do have works published in another book called Dark Knights which was a limited edition from http://www.penmenwritings.org

STACY GOLL
(Alias Norak Drogan)

Circles

I took the one less traveled by
Where others dare not follow
For the danger that awaits
Is unnerving, uncertain
Fear
Once on the path
Once can never return
The path leads forever
An open, never-ending circle
Lost

The one less traveled by
Where the danger awaits
Leading farther away
Finding others, more
Time
Travel infinite paths
Never before tread
Never before seen
Winding through, around
Lost

STACY GOLL

Visions

Now I gently take my leave
Fading away through darken eve
Gliding through shadows dim
Rising by moonlight's glim
Shadows fade through darken light
Slipping through the wisp of night
Many story and song are told
As long forgotten ages unfold
Grasping tight to mother's side
Children watch as fates unhide
Twisting future of vision seen
Showing what could well have been
Hidden by the mist of time
Path of knowledge the finest line
Seeking truth through given fears
Sorrow found with burning tears
Holding back the steps to tread
Journeys long awaited end
As buried secrets come to light
Flowing forth the given sight

Stacy Goll

Yearning

We set upon this path alone
wondering what shall be shown
wandering down the empty road
it takes us to a place unknown.
The place we reach is dead and gone
all but here naught and none
we stand amidst the eternal yearn
to see the truth and knowledge learns.
We stand upon the ground of old
where battles raged and stories told
while wind of fortune whispers cold
with songs of wisps and fae untold.

STACY GOLL

Milena Gomez

Milena Gomez, author of the poetry books Emotions: Love Made Courageous and La Boheme: Melody of Poems has always loved Romance. In her poetry she always tries to blend her real life experiences with nature and a spark of romantic emotion to create different types of poems for every reader. For her there's no better life than being a writer, writing romance, that is. Future works may include novellas, as well as novels. You can visit her at: www.milenagomez.com, where there's always something new!

A Note from the Author, Milena Gomez

When I was a child I always loved to read. I was crazy about books and I couldn't put them down. But I never knew that after leaving Cuba on September 19, 1995 that I would come to love writing books as well. "I'm Cuban American and I'm always going to vote! I'm going to represent my new home."

Yes, books had a positive effect on me and when I read them, I felt joy. But making up stories with my dolls didn't give away any clues about what I wanted to do when I grew up. Reading "*La Edad de De Oro*" *(The Golden Age)* by the famous Cuban hero, poet and children's writer Jose Marti gave me a sign about how wonderful writing could be, until I asked God about my purpose in this world.

Surely, I thought, washing dishes wasn't my talent and that there was more to me than meets the eye. I wasn't wrong. As I moved on to High School I discovered how wonderful it is to write poetry. The first poem in my book: *"Emotions: Love Made Courageous"* was the answer to my prayers. Yet writing just one poem didn't make me happy. I knew I had to write a book and then another one and I did write a book, the second one and on an on!

Between the Lines

Darkness about
Covers the land,
A little girl dreams,
With pen in hand

Unable to see
She continues to write
Ink is her only friend
From her pen, words take flight.

She writes the lines
That shapes all the words,
Hiding no longer,
Her words must be heard.

She puts the pen down
Thought and word she has combined,
Tomorrow in the light of day
Another girl will read between the lines.

Milena Gomez

Today I Fell in Love

Today I fell in love for the first time
I saw its beauty in a couple's glance.

I saw that love comes in many forms,
And that first come friendship, then much more.

Today I felt selfish in many ways
For keeping my poor heart locked away:

Like a fairy tale I have always dreamt
That my blue prince will come to rescue me in the end.

How could I have been so blind to the light?
How could anyone be?

Today I didn't fall in love for the first time
I didn't see its beauty in a couple's glance.

Love is Omnipresent and invisible,
it is more than meets the eye.

MILENA GOMEZ

Young Man

Little boy, you are now a man
You were taught not to cry
To be a hard working man
To take care of your sister
And to grow up fast.

Don't ever cry if you're in pain,
Work hard for your future
and your sister instead!
Stop playing with your toy cars
and see what is real,
Mom and Daddy are gone
and you need to deal...

Little boy, you are more than a man
you cry when you're in pain;
your work is made of love
for your sister instead...

You have grown up so much,
With her time by time
and thinking of it now,
Tomorrow has not crossed your
mind.

You have played with your toy cars,
you and her, together
Mom and Daddy are gone
but they see you from Heaven

knowing how to deal
Is your strongest suit,
Today your sister knows
About happiness because of you!

Milena Gomez

Stephanie Harmon

Stephanie was born and raised in Miami in February 1965. She showed her ability to write poetry and children's stories at an early age and has been writing ever since. Both of Stephanie's parents are Hungarian which is in Eastern Europe. She still has family there. Stephanie is a retired Police dispatcher with almost 20 years of impeccable service. In addition, she was an instructor at the Miami Dade Police Academy in a program written and implemented by herself and a few choice others at the department. Stephanie currently enjoys retirement by spending time writing stories and playing with her Labrador Retrievers.

Church with the White Steeple

I was sleeping so soundly, so deeply, so comfortably. I realized it was the best sleep that I had had for many, many months. I relished it and turned over in bed to grasp more of the phenomenon that was occurring. When I turned over, I made a fatal judgment error. For now, you see, the sun shone in streaks through my bedroom window and subsequently into my eyes. Now I am awakened by sunlight. Right through thick navy blue drapes. As if they weren't even there. Annoying me.

As I made the bed, I debated a new pattern to buy for the windows in the very near future. I made a mental note to buy the thickest curtains available, one that the sun can't permeate. I went down to get the morning newspaper and the mail that had been delivered as well. I figured I could read as I ate my breakfast and maybe find some home improvement sales. Then again, someone once said that aluminum foil on windows blocks out all of the sun's rays and heat too; so I've got that if all else fails.

"Ms. Samantha Hampton 306 South Falls Way, Miami, FL 33311"

Well, a letter to me but from whom? Only one way to find out, I answered myself under my breath. I ripped into the letter and found a beautiful hand written calligraphy note card requesting the honor of my presence on Wednesday, June 10, 2003 at the oldest Christian church in the Redlands called the Church with the White Steeple. I had heard of the old church but I had never seen it or attended any of their services. The church had been on the cover of many magazine covers as well. The invitation specified I arrive precisely at 7:30 P.M. And there was another interesting tidbit enclosed in that letter: a pre-paid, prearranged rented vehicle will be waiting for me in front of my building for me to drive all the way down to the Redlands. "Now this is getting interesting!" I said to my reflection in the mirror.

Wednesday morning I woke up with enthusiasm and went down to see if the car had been dropped off like the note said. I checked with the doorman and in fact, it was there. It was a nice little convertible so I hopped in and put the top down. "Great ride," I said out loud to no one.

I decided to go upstairs and pack a small overnight bag. I brought along a hat and with that, I was on my way.

There was a map left for me on the front seat. I followed the directions with ease. The sun was shining and traffic was light. The farther I traveled, I felt as if I was below sea level. Lower and lower, I began to see marshy side shoulders and acres and acres of wet lands; Beautiful and isolated.

I stopped for a bite to eat at a little outdoor cafe where seagulls waited for a handout.

I felt very aware of my breathing. The air seemed clear and clean. After eating, I did not feel full.

I decided first to drive on to the church to make sure I knew where it was. Then I would check into the hotel.

After driving several miles off South Dixie Highway, I could see the steeple. It emanated a glow high into the sky and in my heart. I knew it was a special place. I turned around in the driveway and made my way to the hotel I passed on the way down.

Upon checking in, I was surprised the concierge had a reservation in my name. "Ms. Samantha Hampton? Here we go," the kind voice rang out.

"Well, thank you," I said. Nothing surprised me at this point. I didn't even know this hotel existed, yet there was a reservation waiting for me.

I freshened up in the room and gave myself a tour of the resort. It was rich and lush and full of flowers. Golfers made their way to and fro and tennis matches were being vigorously played. I just enjoyed the atmosphere.

Before I knew it, it was time for me to head out to the church. I felt rejuvenated and refreshed. I pulled into the driveway as the sun was setting. It was going to be very dark very soon. I walked up the steps to the door and realized the only source of light inside the church was candlelight. It cast a warm and pleasant glow on its parishioners who were peppered throughout the church.

I stopped at the doorway so my eyes could become accustomed to the poor light. A mild mannered man introduced himself as John and welcomed me by name. I was surprised he knew me for I did not know him. John asked me to follow him alongside the pews toward the front of the church. As I walked up to the front, I passed several parishioners. I nodded and smiled, but they ignored me. One after another, I smiled and nodded and was ignored. Strange.

"Don't worry. They aren't responding because they can't see you, Samantha," John said.

I imaged they couldn't see me because of the poor light in the church. I smiled in acknowledgement.

John and I made our way to some seats and I sat down. It gave me an opportunity to look at the congregation as they prepared for the service to commence.

John took his place at the pulpit and immediately I realized it was not to be an ordinary church service.

He introduced himself to the congregation and said he had a special guest. I knew he meant me, but he never mentioned my name. All throughout this journey, everything had been pre-arranged for me. A car, a hotel room and everyone seemed to know who I was and that I was here and yet for the service, no introduction? What's going on here?

Then John walked down the steps from the pulpit and took my hand. We walked over to a young lady sitting on the end in the first row. John held my hand up and placed it on her shoulder.

"Sandra, are you sensing anyone right now?" John asked.

Oh, she's blind, I thought to myself. But why wouldn't John introduce me to Sandra?

Then I looked closer. In the faint light I could see that I knew this woman. I used to work with her many years ago.

I immediately said, "Sandra, its Samantha."

John looked at me and smiled. "She can't hear you or see you, Samantha. But if you think about what you want to say, she may receive your message."

Before I could even digest what John had said, Sandra chimed in, "Oh, it's Samantha, isn't it!"

"Yes, yes," John acknowledged.

Sandra went on, "I used to work with Samantha. She was such a nice young lady. She was very good at her job. The best; everybody liked her. Samantha was a very fair person and kind. Yes, she was very kind, don't you know."

I couldn't believe my ears! Sandra was saying all of this about me and didn't even know that I was there. Why was she saying these nice things? I didn't understand so I looked to John. My eyes filled with tears. "What's going on?" I said.

You'd better sit down," John said. "Now it's about time you hear it from me." My knees started to buckle and sitting down seemed like a good idea. "Have you noticed that you know all of these people here⁹" John inquired. "From some point in your life, these are all acquaintances of yours, non-related."

"Oh, yes. I do recall most of them. What does that mean? What am I doing here?"

"Samantha, if I was to ask your loved ones what they thought of you, what do you think they would say? Good things; Glowing things?" John asked paternally.

"Well. ..."I was at a loss for words.

"Here we inquire about you from those you once knew. Friends, co-workers; the better the response, the better you are looked upon. These are the last words you shall hear about your life on earth from those you knew."

I smiled through tears streaming down my face as I realized that somehow I was in some type of after life transition. It's not easy to get to heaven. You've got to be a nice person and a good person inside. And only God decides if you are chosen.

"Okay, now, where were we," John continued.

As I sat facing a congregation of people I used to know, with the warmth of the candlelight bathing their faces, they could not see me. They could not know why they were speaking of me. Only that John dictated the forum regarding a nice girl named Samantha Hampton who was on her way to heaven.

Stephanie M. Harmon

Beverly Houck

I was born December 1st, 1947, in Ionia Michigan. I was raised on a farm. We were very poor but I did not know it until I went to school in the second grade. My kindergarten was one field away in a one room one teacher school house. We had recess and would go slide down that big farm hill in the winter. When it was time to come in Mrs. Bercha would ring a bell. The bathroom was outside and so cold you had to put on your winter coats to use the facilities. My class size was two and we sat behind the piano and played dominoes.

The other classes which went to the eighth grade used the rest of the building. After that year the old one room school house was torn down. We lived in a tenant house on my grandparent's farm – there was a path worn from our little home to grandma's house. I trod that may times – was welcomed and would help myself to her brown bread and homemade butter. She was always there. I used to play in her button tin – she showed me how to make a button spin between thread or make a button bracelet.

Up the dirt road was my great grandparent's farm down the road was my Uncle Henry's farm. That's how it was back then people stayed and didn't move around like they do today. Family was up a path or down the road. We had no running water or inside bathroom. An old farm cook stove was what my mom used in the winter to cook and heat the downstairs and a small two burner electric stove which sit on a table for summer cooking. The water had to be carried in for all our washing, cooking, baths, which I might add was once a week but we had a wash up every day. We did have electricity. I marvel at my mother's ability to cook, bake and can vegetables from the garden with what she had. A wash day was all day. Pull out the wringer washer, go get the water heat it – sort at least five loads of clothes. You washed the whites first, then by hand put the clothes through a hand wringer into the next tub of rinse water -then run through hang wringer again - then outside to hang on the clothes line. You used that wash water over to do the rest of the wash then the last was the dirty work farm clothes. All day it took. Not done yet. Next day was all the ironing. Didn't have permanent press or thrown away hankies back then. In the winter clothes lines were strung up inside with papers on the floor to catch the drips. Well so much hard work back then for grown-ups.

I was too young to do much. One chore I had was to take water back in the fields (in antique mason jars of today) to my Dad and Grandpa or whoever was working bailing the hay. So hot in those fields – they wore long sleeves, jeans, hats. The sweat would soak the shirts and help cool the skin plus keep the sun from burning their skin. (Sunscreens hadn't been invented yet)

The farm was a place where a child could play in the barn-make a tunnel in the hay. Climb a corn crib. Watch grandpa milk a cow. Sit on a pear tree and eat a pear. Go to the creek take off your shoes pull up your pants and watch or catch polliwogs. Play in the corn field, ride a tractor or best yet up on the very top of a wagon filled with bales of hay going to the barn for winter storage from a long hard work day in the hot fields of late August early September. with my Dad or Grandpa driving the tractor. My other chores were, gather nuts, hickory, black walnuts, butternuts. Sometimes for supper Mom would send me out to gather wild asparagus which grew in a corner of a field.

I loved that farm and I am sad that my girls will not know or experience that way of living for it is gone for no more generations to know. I was married at seventeen and will be married forty years this November. I have three girls – all married – three grandchildren one on the way. YEY!

Hobbies – Garden and flowers collecting antiques. I have two of my great grandfather's wagon wheels in my backyard with ivy growing around and up the trees. I have peonies that my grandmother had in her garden and have passed some on to each daughter. I love my back yard.

I have had painful experiences in my life but I know God made one as well as the other and he does not waste pain. I have written them down and maybe someday I can share my experience strength and hope with someone and just maybe help them.

I did not know and am still in awe of how God brings talents out in us at different times of our life if we just yield to him. I was fifty six before I picked up a pen and put it to paper and I have no formal education. At family birthdays I write each one a little poem or story and now every one wants one. I read them out loud and tears will come to their eyes. I have an endless supply of subjects and ideas that fill my head. God has led me on a journey and I'm not done yet for I feel he has more in store. I have more to learn and I pray and grow in this new found me. Do I dare dream? Thanks for your interest. May God Bless!

Medical Records Mouse in the Corner

Records! Records! Records!

That's where it's all at. Numbers all put together. For people they represent! A test here, one there! Take a picture put it where! Storage they say, send it to Medical Records. They know what to do. Quite the job with all that goes on in a hospital - people sick in and out. Doctors and nurses running about, taking care of patients all in different ways; What is needed will be done, then write it down, doctors will dictate and then another team kicks in, type the dictations - next team - right through the door.

Each team member has a job and knows how it all must go in the computer. It's quite a busy place with phone calls for information – who knows all kinds of people call, all with a different purpose. Each patient has a file, there own place, through the door next, you will see Eight Tall Movable Files 10,000 Alone! Keeps you busy! Keeping tract of all these patients' misery, sickness, pain, surgery, x-rays, meds, new babies born and everything else that goes on till the wee early morning; could be one hour or several days.

Keep it straight! Keep it straight! No Fret! Not to worry! Add more to do. That's when the code team takes over, more responsibility, new laws, need those codes to do the bills, I guess the insurance company wants to know. OH Boy here we go. And there is allot more I don't know.

If records are not right and Doctors miss a signed line;

Guess who catches all those must do's and don't do's? Medical Records

Keep it straight knows the terms who signs what – someone is at the door. It's a person with a request of a record that is stored. Well this team is on there toes, they can answer all those woes, make a copy of what they need. Help that person feel at ease.

They are not just a number but a human being with thoughts and feelings and a name. Some had life's pain and came to a hospital for a stay, for some care and answers. The girls have done a job well done. For the people leave with papers in their hand and sometimes a smile for they have been treated with caring and dignity with quite some style.

There is more to the unseen eye in Medical Records another part, in a different spot - that has to be done - keep tract of all those Doctors - papers in order - keep those licenses up to date, I'm sure there is more to reiterate.

This team is all over the place working – here – there – every where not together in the same spot, but all together as a team !

Medical Records is quite the place, you should be a little mouse in this space and see all they do. We should say, "Thank you." in appreciation to the team from the TOP all the way through, for everyone in this department. For this little mouse has eyes that doubled in size of what a Team in Medical Records has to do and I'm sure I did not see it all, but Oh Boy what I did has sparked my AWE.

Beverly Houck

New Beginnings God's Healing

A new day begins and a sad day flees
There is sunshine today and green trees
A breeze comes and flows it smells of spring
Not so bad today the problem I had yesterday
Because I've done the best I can with what I know & who I am
I will be glad to laugh this day and live for no more yesterdays
The winds blow grasses and trees they sway
They flow and move and it's ok.
My mind is free when I dig and plant flowers with thee
There is a peace that comes
A mind set free from all misery
I will blend flowers dig in the earth
Work as many as I can
Each year – new flowers that vary
Some flowers are pink some are white
Some that are small will grow and be tall
Some hang over and spark your awe
They are all beautiful each one is unique
No matter how you plant them
They may surprise you how they peak
When summer is done & this spring must end
It's sad to see this beauty end
If God grants a new spring
It will start over again
It is important my friend to remember
This is a special gift
It comes from God it is a blessing
We must give thanksgiving
To a springs new beginning and God's ever healing!

BEVERLY HOUCK
Romans 5:3-5
We also rejoice in our sufferings, because we know that suffering produces perseverance;
Perseverance, character; and character, hope.
And hope does not disappoint us, because God has poured out his love into our hearts by the Holy Spirit, whom he has given us.

Precious Feet

See these little feet of ten weeks
God's precious gift of life
They hold something in store
When they grow they can open a door
Did you know they are a human being
Some new mom said, "Oh no, not me
I can not have a new baby you see
I don't have time - It's not in my plan
It will not work – No one must know
I have much to do – I'm really scared
No time for the new little you."
What must I do – Where do I go
Who's this talk of God – I don't know
Easy way out (the devil whispers)
Won't take much time - It will be gone
Some of God's people are here to help
Please don't do this – This precious life will grow
God has a plan for this new life don't you know
Come let us show you a new way
We want to show you a picture
Of what's inside you
Little Feet - Ten toes – Look they move
This child has a heart and it beats
Please don't listen to the evil one
He does not tell you what grief will come
There will be guilt deep inside you
Pain and much despair
Just wait a short time
We can show you a new way
God has sent us here to be with you today
To help you along your journey
The evil one will tear you down
There is nothing but trouble when he whispers in your ear
Our arms are open wide
We will keep you secure
Oh by the way there is a blessing coming your way

Please don't throw it away
Those little feet will be walking someday
Those little feet will bring you a smile
Those little feet will bring warmth and love
Those little feet are a gift from above

Beverly Houck

Michael Levy

Michael Levy is the author 6 books. His new book is titled: "The Joys of Live Alchemy." The words "Live Alchemy" are an anagram of Michael's name. His web site is ranked number one in the world out of 3,500,000 websites when "Inspirational books" are the search words on Google.

Web Sites: http://www.pointoflife.com
E-mail: mikmikl@aol

White Cap Warriors

It was a calm morning,
the ocean glistening
with magnificent sparking diamond,
uncountable treasures,
there to be savored, by the ob-servant eye,
Suddenly a blast of cold air sprung up,
armies of white caps began their assault
wave after wave of infantry,
apparently, all with a purpose,
seemingly, on an important mission,
Their supremacy could not be halted,
I tried to fathom their cause
why did they destroy the diamond treasures,
that innocently brought such pleasure,
unceasingly, they formed their groups
advancing, so they thought,
Their journey was not smooth
rather, rough and chaotic
onward, towards the final destination,
a simple shoreline, that just enjoyed
its place in the sun,
finding no objective to their quest, the white caps
vanished into nothingness,
just like belligerent human beings.

Michael Levy

Ralph Lichtenberger

Ralph was born in Illinois on July 27, 1955. He is of Hungarian decent, having both his mother and father's family tree originating there.

He has had a flawless career as a Driver Engineer with the Coral Gables Fire Department, retiring with 30 years of service.

He lives with his wife, Lourdes in Miami. With a schedule busier than that of the normal work week, the two of them also enjoy traveling together on the road in their RV.

Dream or Premonition?

It was the summer of August, 1988. My friend and I at work were talking about our South Florida boating experiences. My friend, Richard and I are avid boatmen, and scuba divers. We've both owned our boats. Rich had a 22 foot open fisherman, and I had a 20 foot open fisherman. We always went out to the outer reefs diving, camping, and fishing. We've known each other for 15 years, and had many years of boating experience.

One day at work, Rich talked about taking a few of his friends out for a dive trip. It's a beautiful dive out there. The outer reef is about 40 to 60 feet deep; A safe depth for all scuba divers. Crystal clear turquoise colored water, with beautiful coral reef heads along with colorful fish, sea fans, and old artifacts about. It was such fun looking for that old Spanish treasure which always eluded us. That was one of the lures for us concerning scuba diving, and boating. We both made plans for Richard's dive trip, and we went over them with a fine toothed comb. Insuring that time, distance, fuel, supplies, and equipment were all up to par. I was not invited on this dive trip, however we always consulted each other on anything pertaining to places to dive, weather conditions, and safety. We are Professional Firefighters and knew Mother Natures' strange ways at times on the high seas. Even in perfect weather, it can turn into a hurricane at a moments notice. Being experienced boatmen and divers, we were always careful of such things. Anyway, Rich had set up his dive trip with his three friends for a pleasurable day of scuba diving. After our shift day, we parted work as usual. Saying good-bye, and keep in touch. We have two days off after each duty day and plenty of time off to enjoy life.

However, that night at home I had a dream or premonition; I had woken up late, and called Rich to explain my dream to him. I had spoken to him for some time explaining everything in my dream. Afterwards, we had left that subject speaking about *his* dive trip plans. Well, we said goodnight to each other, and all was well. As we hung up the phone, I was still very concerned however. I didn't think he had grasped the importance of my concern for him. One day later Rich and I reported to work as usual. I couldn't help to convey my concern to him all day long. I said, "Rich, I had a bad dream the other night." I told him, "Your boat came down to see you." I said. The same thing I had told him over the phone the night I called him. As I remember it, my dream was that Rich had gone out to sea with his three friends. They had a great day. Suddenly, as all four divers were on the bottom of the reef, about 45 feet deep, his boat had sunk, and had drifted down engine first to meet them on the bottom just a few feet away from their position. The boat, as I saw it in my dream had sunk with the outboard motor just touching the bottom. The bow pointing upward at a 45 degree angle; Weather conditions were perfect. The area of the dive was just off Fowey Rocks Light House. Rich and I have many hours of dive time there without a hitch. And as a weather buff, I'm used to monitoring the weather here in South Florida for any possible severe storms, or predictions.

Well, it was Richard's last day at work before his annual leave. He was going on a short vacation of one week to enjoy his time off, and his dive trip with his friends. We parted work the next day as usual. "Have a good trip Rich." I said. And, "Keep in touch." Three days went by. I went to work as usual. Rich was out on his boat by this time with his friends. I thought about him often. I shrugged my dream off as being a fluke. I actually forgot about it, since Rich never called me. I knew he was out for only one day. But, I still wondered why he never called after three days.

One night 4 days later, I get a call from Richard. It was about 10:00 at night. When I answered the phone he said, "Hey, Ralphie!" as usual. I said, "Hey Rich, how'd it go?" Then it hit, and hit hard. He had said in a strange laughing manner, "Ralph, your dream came true." I said, "What?" He had said, "The boat came down to see me, Ralph." There was a long moment of silence on the phone. I couldn't believe what I've just heard. Yet, he spoke of everything I've told him in my dream. Everything I had told Rich in my dream was on the mark, and true. He had said the boat came down to see him, sinking in the same place, time, and manner as I had told him it would in my dream. In other words, my dream came true. Richard and his three friends had seen what had happened. They were in the water for 18 hours before the Coast Guard located them for rescue. That's why I didn't hear from Rich. He was in trouble. Yet, I had no idea what was happening at the time, nor felt anything was wrong. The Coast Guard had rescued them, and Richards's boat was finally salvaged at a cost of $800.00 from the sea. They had lost all their gear including cameras, dive gear, electronics, and safety equipment, not to mention the boat itself. Richard told me, "If it wasn't for our buoyancy compensators, we could not have stayed afloat for that length of time. They had dropped their weight belts, and with the little air remaining in their scuba tanks were able to float freely on the surface in hopes of being seen for rescue. They stayed with the boat, as required. They were all saved. Tired, and weather beaten, but safe. Thank God. Since that time, Richard has retired from the Fire Service. He now resides in Wisconsin; Far from the ocean, and boats. I believe dreams do come true. This was my first and only premonition. Why did it happen? Rich and I had talked about all the possibilities, and scenarios. Was the boat swamped by a passing boater? Was the boat swamped by a rouge wave? Was the boat plug inadvertently forgotten to be installed? Since all the crew members were under water at the time, and the boat was left unattended no one will ever know.

However, the case remains the same. I dreamed it, and then it happened. Why did I have this particular dream? Why did Richard not heed my warning? For God only knows.

Ralph Lichtenberger

My Dream

Somewhere in a destroyed small town in some unfamiliar place only the ruined foundations linger. An apparent war or disaster of some kind must have occurred there. A green grassy hilly land where only two armed guards dressed in khaki uniforms with black gun belts stood around. Being too far away to hear, I could not decipher their language. The men were laughing, so I thought they were telling jokes to each other.

I was being held for some unknown reason. I just knew I was an innocent victim of some unknown event. A block away, a few two story warehouses stand that cover about four city blocks. There I was in an unknown predicament in a mysterious place. Wearing rags for clothes and walking around aimlessly among the ruins, wondering my fate under the strict supervision of the guards.

Suddenly in the midst of a diversion out of the clear blue sky, I had the chance to escape the clutches of my captors. As the guards walked ahead of me scurrying for cover, I ran in the opposite direction. I ran and ran over the grassy hills and ruins. I came to the warehouse section where I ran down the alley. Looking behind me to assure myself the guards were not chasing me.

As I came to the end of the block there was a three foot black vinyl covered chain link fence which bordered a trailer park. Looking from side to side and behind me to make sure I was not being chased. The trailer park was a familiar sight since I had once lived in one. Ahead of me was a wooded tree grove with a narrow gravel walkway.

As I could feel myself running faster and faster, I began to lift off the ground in flight. I was not amazed I was flying since I had done this before. I just didn't know when it was going to happen again. Nevertheless, I was very glad to be flying since this would assure my escape. I was flying at an altitude of about 15 feet and going approximately as fast as 20 miles per hour. I approached a wooded tree grove with a narrow gravel walkway.

As I flew above and followed this trail suddenly I noticed a little black boy wearing a colorful horizontally striped shirt riding his new bicycle. The young boy was looking at me through his glasses with pure amazement and pointed at me as he commented to himself that I was flying. I looked down at him and smiled.

I have a very good sense of direction and wanted to fly southeast in the direction of my home. Fighting to control this heading since an unidentified force kept trying to alter my course to the northwest. It was energy like a magnet pulling me. I came close to losing control several times however I always regained control. I overcame the force and continued flying until darkness fell.

Finally a populated small town was within site. Slowing down and loosing some altitude, I came to an intersection of small wood framed houses and businesses. The street lights were glistening brightly. There were people standing and others were sitting in front of an establishment. It was hard to decipher the sign on the building. The people commented and pointed at me as I flew by.

Another small black boy was coming out of the establishment. He was all alone and walked to the middle of the street eating something and carrying a bag. Unexpectedly for some unidentified cause I had some difficulty controlling my flight loosing altitude. Inadvertently I was heading directly towards the young child wearing a short sleeved t-shirt and with a clean cut ebony black hair. He did not see me and I tried desperately not to crash into him. Despite my maximum effort, I grazed his head lightly with my foot. The young boy was not seriously hurt, but he was in a daze. The accident stirred up the people in the surrounding. They started yelling as I flew away.

Once again flying and gaining altitude I was afraid to be recognized and risk the chance of captivity. I flew above a narrow brick-laid street sort of Old Key West style, trees surrounding both sides and power lines to my left. Looking down I viewed more old structures, street light and more trees.

As I passed one building with a picture framed window, a glass store front and a tree partially covering my view, came a police officer. As I flew past him about fifteen feet above the ground, he noticed me and scurried to the middle of the street pointing at me. Once again sensing the fear I had experienced in more than one occasion. This police officer was wearing the same uniform as the guards that had me confined a while back.

It was a struggle trying aimlessly to gain more altitude to change course due to buildings on both sides and power lines just above. The only way to fly was forward so I proceeded knowing that I had to turn sooner or later. Finally I noticed up ahead a large gap between the power lines. Three power lines were strung from pole to pole at about three feet apart. I veered to the left gaining a little altitude. As my head and body got closer, the thick black wires were getting closer.

The closer I ventured to the heavy black wires, the harder I prayed that I would make it through. I made it this far and I did not want to loose now. For some reason I flew inverted between the top and middle wires, crossing over the treetops and buildings. I remember missing the wires coming about four inches away from my chest.

This maneuver made me very nervous, but I had faith I would succeed, which I did. I remember thanking God for I had survived. Continuing to fly and gaining altitude again during what was by now a dark clear night, I felt free. At this moment I heard a voice say to me, "It's a good thing you gained altitude because the power lines surround the block and you would have flown right into them." That's when I woke up.

Ralph Lichtenberger

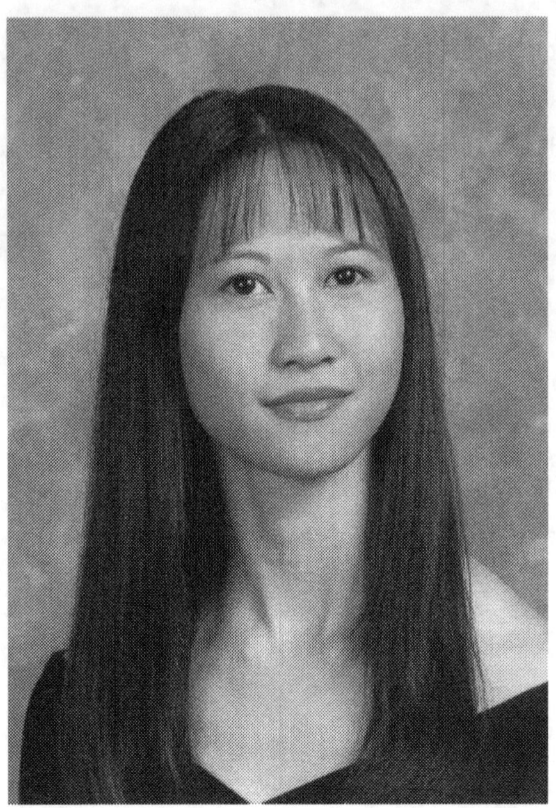

Adrienne Lin

At the age of seven, Adrienne Lin moved from Vietnam to the United States with her mother and her two older brothers. Because she was the only one who could go to school, she became the family translator and connection to anything that was English speaking. Adrienne began writing stories as soon as she learned English and has marveled at how effectively she is able to communicate through the written word. Adrienne Lin is currently attending Stanford University to major in Economics and minor in English Literature.

Crane Flies

Crane flies
are like
daddy long-legs with wings
are like
filmy, stretched pieces of
black cotton, suspended
like nets over tables
at the restaurant
I went to last night,
a lazy roof to keep
out the bugs and birds.

Crane flies
are like
single feathers with legs,
oh ugly gray, black
feathers torn and worn
sifting through the air
Floating up and down
up and down
up and down
and I, I cringe with trepidation
body and face buried beneath my covers,
watching daddy long-legs with wings,
torn ugly feathers with legs,
hovering over me.

ADRIENNE LIN

9th Row

Halfway through the concert she leaned over and told him she was hungry. Before he realized it, his eyebrows and cheek muscles had twisted in a way that suggested a hint of annoyance. He quickly melted it into a polite smile. "Wait until the concert is over," he told her. She hesitated for a few ambivalent seconds, then leaned back in her chair, breathing rather deliberately as her fingers loosened its grip on the armrest. The pianist played on for several minutes before she leaned over again and said, in a quiet urgency, "No, now."

He sighed. The tickets which he had worked hard to procure had cost over three hundred dollars. Tonight, the two blue slips of paper bought them a seat in the coveted ninth row of an exquisitely elegant and handsome concert hall. The seats, decked in a velvety red, formed arched rows running all the way to the back of the house. Further back from where they sat and at least twenty feet above the floor of the first level, the balcony nested still more people.

A few slight movements of the head and he was able to observe a full house of sophisticatedly attired men and women. The women sat straight; their backs lined with the back of the chairs, hands folded over crossed legs. The men, most of them in suits, held programs with one arm with the other on the armrest. The people sat in a mesmerized silence, eyes keenly fixed on the dancing fingers of Mr. John Baltorie. On the ceiling above the stage was reflected the movements of his hands, a phenomenon caused by the combination of the lights and the fine piano.

"Jake, I'm hungry," she said, slicing the silence with her strained feminine voice.

"I know, we'll get something as soon as the concert is over."

"Jake, I want to leave."

"Yes, in a while."

"No, now."

"Yes, in a while."

She hesitated as before and leaned back in her chair. He gazed at her with a puzzled look, trying to decipher her irrational urgency. She ignored him and simply stared blankly forward. He shrugged and gave his jacket a little tug before leaning back into his own seat, becoming suddenly aware of the music. Once again he began to relax and re-enter the enchantment of the pianist when out the corner of his eye he saw her reach down to the floor and pick up her purse. She stood up suddenly, and, excusing herself, made her way across the rows of seated people, the hand clutching the purse waved in the air for balance, while the other ruffled the backs of the chairs in front of her. A man let out repressed growl as her heel dug through his shoe, and the people in the row in front turned around at the commotion.

"Janie!!" he half called, half whispered to her over the music of the piano and the collective glare of the audience. But she kept walking, trampling and navigating through the dark forest of feet and legs, and all this while the piano sang. Her black dress, though previously plain and conspicuous in the dark, shimmered as she moved. Taken by shock and embarrassment, he stood up and followed her, apologizing helplessly while men and women murmured in annoyance. In this way, they painfully made their way across the audience to the door, their bodies' irregular silhouettes against the lit stage.

So much for the coveted ninth row to procure the longest path possible...

* * * *

Outside in the car they sat in silence, neither one speaking or wanting to. Or, rather, she did not want to speak, and he did not know what to say and did not want to be the first to speak. But the longer it sat, the more the silence billowed out and pushed the air out of the car, making it hard to breathe. He cleared his throat, coughed twice, and slowly said, "Why did you do that?"

"Do what?" she answered, rather carelessly.

"What? Do what? You know exactly what you did. Why did you run out like that, making such a scene?"

"Where do you want to go?" she asked.

"Janie, why did you run out like that?"

She didn't answer but instead stared at the windshield. She put her elbow on the little ledge where the base of the window met the door and flung the side of her head into her hand. "I was hungry," she said.

"Oh, dear God, so you were hungry!" he exclaimed, breathing hard and twisting his upper body violently so that he faced her, arms flailing. "So you were hungry and you just ran out like that, just stood up in the middle of his piece and ran over feet and chairs to the door, ignoring me and swinging the door open without the least thought, letting in that bright block of light piercing into the concert hall. You did all that just because you were hungry!"

She took her arm off the window ledge and folded both of them across her chest in a somewhat petulant manner. "I told you I was hungry. I told you I was starving, and I told you I wanted to leave. *You* didn't listen because *you* chose not to hear."

"I did hear you!" He put both of his hands over his eyes and dragged them down his face, trying to hold in his temper. "I did hear you, but apparently you couldn't wait until the concert was over."

He expected a snappy retort from her but none came. She just put her elbow on the ledge of the window and returned to her original position. He waited again but she did not speak. He leaned his head back on the headrest and closed his eyes.

His face was flushed from the conversation and he was breathing heavily. He could see the embarrassment of their exit from the concert on his eyelids. He was upset not because the tickets had been so expensive or that he had gone through so much trouble to secure them, but because he had been thinking of his grandmother at the moment Janie stood up. He remembered sitting next to her, his two chubby legs dangling from the piano bench and his two fingers placed on two keys on the piano, one black and the other white. Sitting like that, he would wait for her signal, and when she nodded he would push down on the two keys simultaneously and complete the melody that she would play. The piano was old and the smell of the wood, though pleasant, never became indistinct. He sat like this with his grandmother on many rainy afternoons, on snowy mornings, on silent nights, on any day, and waited to push the two keys, the sound of which elated him when it rung together with the string of notes his grandmother made.

His grandmother died when he was a boy of nine. At a funeral, they hired a pianist to play. He had perfect hands, fingers untouched by arthritis, and he moved around the piano with ease. But every time I heard him play my two notes, my stomach twisted and I swallowed the choking in my chest.

"So why are we still sitting here?" she asked.

He pulled in his breath. "Okay, fine," he said, "Where do you want to go to eat?"

"I don't know," she said. "I'm not really hungry."

Adrienne Lin

Stains

When I look back on my childhood, I see fuzzy teddy bears, turtle-shaped pools, birthday candles that never blow out, and my mother running toward us with a meat cleaver. Sometimes, I can even see a puddle image of my father, drunken and so foul that I can almost smell him. But my mother I can always see vividly—the dirty brown hair loosely tied near the back of the neck, wisps of the tangled mop always about her face, the frail hand gripping the cleaver.

The day that my mother ran towards us with the meat cleaver I was in a green inflatable pool with my sister Amy and my brother Dave. The pool was shaped like a turtle. It even had four stubs protruding from the sides and one in the front to signify the head. I remember arguing about who was going to be the shark, who was going to be the fleeing fish, and who was going to be the drunken sailor who had fallen overboard. Amy called this game Shark Attack, although it may as well have been called Dave Attack because Dave always got what he wanted, and he was always the shark.

I was the first one to see my mother that day. She walked out of the door and stood on the patio in her green and brown speckled dress, staring at something to the side of the house. The wind ran its fingers through her hair and billowed her dress so that her head and hands seemed too small for her body. I watch her standing still for a long time. As she turned to face the pool the light caught something by her leg and I saw the cleaver calmly held by her side. Slowly she placed one foot on the top step and descended the stairs one step at a time.

The sun was bright that day and I distrusted my eyes. Streams of thoughts raced through my head as I watched her. I couldn't understand why my mother would go outside with a cleaver in her hand. I waited for Amy and Dave to notice her but neither of them said anything. Dave was too busy gnawing on my arm and Amy darted back and forth in the pool like an oblivious fish. I continued staring at my mother as she coolly stepped over the lime green garden hose. As soon as she walked past the hose she started to run, the cleaver held in mid-air. Her hair flew wildly and the veins bulged from the firm grip around the wooden handle. Frantically I began punching Dave. I pushed his forehead back with my hand but still his teeth clung tightly to my arm. I kicked him in the stomach, my unclipped toenails raked across his skin. He fell backwards, dazed. The upper half of his body landed outside the pool and he laid there crushing the air in the turtle as water flowed past him onto the grass.

When Dave finally caught sight of my mother, he let out a long, shrill shriek. The sound froze the cells in our muscles. Amy's head popped up from underneath the water. She wiped her wet bangs from her goggles. Her mouth slowly dropped and the water from her hair and face dripped into it. Then both Amy and Dave lunged at me and seized my arms. We let out a scream that spiraled upward and rattled the leaves on the trees. My mother only ran faster. The gleaming cleaver caught the light of the sun and fried it like water on a hot skillet. Amy started to cry and squeezed my stomach until I couldn't breathe. I wanted to get up and run but we were all paralyzed with a fear that pinned us to the ground—a fear that if we stood up we would die quicker. I felt Dave's teeth dig into my arm again; his hot tears mixing with the fear on my skin.

The day that my mother ran toward us with the meat cleaver she tripped over a rock just before she reached the pool and fell face down on the grass. The cleaver fell on the neck of the turtle and the air from the punctured head violently hissed out. I pushed Amy and Dave out of the pool and we stumbled away on hands and knees, running and crawling and not waiting to catch our balance. The sun had heated up the pavement and it burned our feet as we staggered into the rosebushes and rock beds.

It was near the steps to the patio that Dave's flailing arms outran his short, chubby legs and his foot got caught in the rocks that lined the path to our backdoor. He fell and his hands and knees scraped against the concrete; the skin opened up and the blood oozed. I saw Amy start to run to him but I yanked open the door and shoved her through it. Then I ran back to Dave and pulled him up the steps.

Once locked inside my room Dave ran to my bed and wedged himself feet first under it, whimpering as he covered his eyes with his hands. Amy collapsed onto the floor and clutched her chest. She cried so hard that she let out half hiccupping, half sobbing noises. Her shoulders jumped up and down. Her mouth was open and lips stretched against her teeth. I kneeled down beside Amy and pulled her small body onto my lap. I held her head to my chest, pulled the goggles off her face, and stroked her wet, brown hair while her convulsions shook both of us. I squeezed her tightly in my arms but she kept shaking, and I shook too as I looked over at my bed and saw that my brother's blood had made fresh stains on the white carpet. I looked down and saw the red indents of Dave's teeth on my arm.

That was the day we all cried, even the house. I know because heard it moan. I heard it cry for the fights and arguments that we had and those that we should have had but never did. I heard it weep for the family that wasn't to be. I heard the lies fall and shatter. I even heard mother cry for the first time in my life.

Amy tells me that our mother was crazy, but I tell her my mother was pitiful. When I think back to it, I think it was the confinement of the lonely house in combination with the perpetually drunken husband and the way we all tried so hard to pretend that we were just another happy family that finally pushed her to the edge. It was the fact that our father was never home, because he was always on trips, in meetings, out with friends, or else he had businesses to take care of, people to see, and important things to do. At least that's what my mother always said to keep up the lies that were indeed a normal family. No, not just a normal family, but a *fine* family. But my mother always forgot to mention that my father always reeked of old, stale alcohol—a smell so strong and nauseating that it lived in his clothes. She forgot to explain why sometimes, when we were in our beds at night, we hear the sound of dishes thrown and broken and slaps on human flesh that ring like gunfire in our ears. Mother also forgot to mention why the police came one night and why my father didn't come home for three days. But then again he was never really home.

Amy also tells me of the time when my mother and father took her to the supermarket to buy food to send me to camp. She tells me that they were arguing a lot that day. They couldn't decide between sugarless gum and gummy bears, Pop Tarts and granola. I have listened to Amy tell me about this trip many times, but the description of it has always been so foreign to me that I have never been able to grasp it. It's because when I try to remember my parents together in one image my mind turns void and my head spins. I see nothing because I can only see them as separate people in their own separate frames.

My mother made sure that the house we lived in had a perfect green lawn accentuated by a white picket fence. She even hired a man to trim the lawn every weekend. In fifth grade, I learned that this was what they called the Suburban Dream—the green lawn, the white fence, the A-frame house, the image of the American family dining together. But Mother didn't understand that you can't make a house, that you can't make a family, and that you can't just throw a blanket over everything and call it *something*.

The realization that my father wasn't coming home anymore came to me unexpectedly and abruptly when Dave and I were digging for worms in the backyard. I remember sticking the broken tree branch into the dirt and flinging out turfs of grass when it came to me that he wasn't on one of those extended trips. Suddenly I couldn't remember when I had last seen him. It made me mad. I was infuriated that he had just casually slipped out of our lives without any of us realizing it—that he had not been there at all but still could slip out. But you couldn't have blamed me for not realizing it, either. We were used to his not being home and my mother telling us he had businesses to take care of. Even after he had been gone for a year she never talked about it.

We hid so many things behind our eyelids and lips. We saw things but didn't talk about anything. We just let them happen and run over us. We never talked about the fact that my father was a cruel alcoholic, never talked about how the house was just a lampshade that covered our beaten family, and we never talked about my father leaving. We just played along with Mother's game, trying to believe that we were a wonderfully happy family. We let the changes gradually slip into our lives like we let our father slip out.

We have never talked about that day with our mother, not since it happened and not even at her death. We just sort of got up the next morning and went about our lives as if that day had never existed. But the memory of it is forever engraved in our minds and we still acknowledge it. When I came down the stairs that night I walked in the kitchen and saw vegetables by the sink and fresh corn on the cob sitting on the cutting board. Some of them were peeled but others still had their leaves and stalks attached. My mother was making dinner, I thought. She was cutting corn for us when something happened and she ran out the door. The entire day has been churning over and over in my head and replaying itself for so many years. I don't believe that my mother knew what she was doing. I don't believe that she wanted to kill us. But Amy disagrees. Amy tells me that if my mother had not tripped on the rock that day we would have all died. Amy tells me every time that my mother was crazy. She tells me that on that day my mother was carrying a cleaver in one hand and insanity in the other.

But Amy doesn't know that our mother is the saddest woman that I have ever known. Amy didn't look out the window that day and see my mother lying there on the wet grass, chest and shoulders heaving up and down from the force of her tears, the right hand still on the cleaver, and the green deflated head of the turtle lying by its side. I don't know how she did it, but my mother lived and died all at the same time. I wanted to help her but in many ways I looked and lived with her at a distance.

Adrienne Lin

Miriam Lorenzo

Miriam Lorenzo was born in Havana, Cuba on April 7, 1950. Her zodiac sign is Aries. Miriam Lorenzo is the founder of Lorenz Skin Center since 1979. Many ladies and gentlemen benefit from professionalism and hard work. Miriam specializes in facials, treating, stretch marks, waxing, peeling, electroderma and electrolysis. Her hobby is writing poetry. She enjoys dancing, listening and interacting with others. Miriam is a "people" person.

Past, Present, Future

Don't think about tomorrow
That tomorrow has been written
In a book that no one has ever read
Think about the present
How you will make up your mind
Thinking about the past – for what?
The past is past

The *future* is…
A question mark
?

The *present* is…
An exclamation point
!

The *past* is…
Forgotten

The Future
Whoever thinks about the *future* is mistaken
The more you force the future –
Furthest from reality it is
Discover that you cannot draw or paint it
To make it please and fit

The Present
The *present* is full of reality
Full of expression and exclamation
Overabundance of impossible things
That cannot be controlled
Occurrences simply have to unfold
Forcing the battle of the impossible
Cannot be changed by pounding
Not even with a kiss
It is incomprehensible

Sleepless at night
Due to life's strife
If you have money you cannot sleep
Because it might get stolen
Worse than allergies from pollen
If you have no money
You cannot sleep trying to find it
To earn more – work more you must commit
Rich or poor will suffer
The agony of cancer that no money can cure
Rough waves will make you tougher
Turbulence one must endure

The Past
If at birth the future was known
The past would have changed so
Experiences and mistakes
Would have not been full blown
Then the performance of a lifetime
Would be richer than Bordeaux
Words of advice – known in advance
With the experience that helped us grow
Would have been grander than a
Priceless gift with a silk bow
The awful things and bad occurrences
From the past must be forgotten
While the good memories from the past sweeten
Therefore, the past equals love
The present is equivalent to reality
While the future ends us all with death

Written in 1979

MIRIAM LORENZO

Sandra R. Mainer

Sandra R. Mainer is the daughter of Clara M. Hymes. She was born and raised in Miami, Florida. She has one daughter named Alexis Alexander. Sandra has been teaching for two years. In her spare times she enjoys spending time with her family, reading and shopping.

My Comfort Zone

Cozy, comfortable….my comfort zone!!! It was in this place where I felt my safest. Many nights, I slept my best. Eighteen years in this house and this is the only room I choose to stay in the most. My goodness, when I was carrying my child, this was the only place she would be her calmest. I went into labor in this very same room. Here I am 27 years old, and all I ever want to do is be in this room. I am afraid of leaving this comfort zone because it is the only one I have ever known. Here I am now a Mother, and my child and I both have found comfort in this same room. This is the one room she has spent so many of her nights and days in that now she feels that it is hers just as much as it is mine. Both, my daughter and I have our own rooms that we could call our place of comfort, but we still choose to be in this room. It is in this room that our family bond and becomes one. This is the room where I choose to be because my best friend is there…my MOMMY'S room!!!

Sandra R. Mainer

Ana Monnar

Ana Monnar was born on March 6, 1954 in Havana, Cuba. She is the oldest of four children. She moved to Miami, Florida at age seven where she still resides with her three children, two dogs and one parrot. She also feeds four stray cats.

Ana Monnar earned a Masters Degree in the area of Early Childhood and Elementary Education from Florida International University. Mrs. Monnar has been teaching for more than 25 years. She is currently teaching fourth grade reading/language arts and is the grade-level chairperson.

Beauty of Haiti

Silk and ribbons clouding the sky
Coastline and beaches – pure black sand
Walking, skipping, splash-splash snorkeling
Good, honest people – giving hand
Flawless beaches, nature walks too
Mountains and forests, trees and shrubs
Rugged valleys, crystal clear bays
Gifts of wisdom from the cherubs
Visitors welcomed to Haiti
Echoes of Africa airing
Panoramic view of realm
Haitian Saints singing and working
Beauty of Haiti is dancing
With the rainbow's pastel colors
Different shades to please the Heavens
Family, good friends and neighbors
Rich – poor; "Where is the middle class?"
Flesh clings tenaciously to mom
Creole speaking, dining delight
Tourist and rich folks under palm
Midnight blue sky, shimmering lights
Stars shining brightly upon moon
Happiness, sadness and sorrow
Hoping to see their loved ones soon
Poor human beings – young and old
Stomach growling, eyes tell it all
Sincerity, dignity, poise
Beauty of Haiti is for all

Ana Monnar

Heart of Gold

To know, to feel and undergo
The heart is richer than gold
It reaches far – also near
The ones you love – young and old

The heart feels and senses true love
Clear as a blue sky – compassion, care
Respect, trust, consideration too
Fearless of love – the bold always dare

The heart is worth more than riches
It holds the key to the Heavens above
Spirit and mind to help others more
To find your soul mate – that will be love

To identify and recognize when love comes
The heart will pound forever more
Adore, admire, value, confide, belief
During waking hours, nights and snore

Who cares about cars or status quo!
Important values and care are the treasures
That a loyal heart will win you over and over
Experience the pleasure of security's measures

Ana Monnar

Will You Love Me Enough?

Will you love me enough? – Today
And tomorrow – when the sun meets
The sea in every horizon
Twirling opportunity's sweets

Will you love me enough? When the
Moon meets infinite brilliant stars
When my hair turns gray from worries
And we go through a dozen cars

Time flying by – ever so sweet
Talking, hugging, and kissing
Wishing more time available
For further clever plannning

Talking daily on the cell phone
Smiling and glowing happily
Merry, blissful, in high spirits
Precious moments come easily

Will you love me enough? When
Green valley meets rugged mountain
And our shadows dance
Then dash and splash in the fountain

Will you love me enough? If fate
Comes knocking – it is meant to be
Destiny is calling
Providence prevails – can you see

Will you love me enough – will I?
We will, love each other enough

Ana Monnar

Melissa Oharriz

Melissa Oharriz was born on June 7, 1984 in Miami, Florida to William and Mirta Oharriz. She graduated from Sts. Peter and Paul Catholic School in 1998 and went on to attend La Salle and American Senior High Schools. She graduated from American Senior in 2002. While in high school Melissa participated in both the school newspaper and the Voices of American the school's choir. During her senior year she was given the honor of "Who's Who Amongst America's Teenagers" for her scholastic achievements. She is now enrolled at Miami Dade College North Campus and is majoring in Vocal Performance.

Melissa was already an accomplished poet by the time she was twelve having her first poem, *"Hold On"* published. Since then she has written many poems including: *Overcoming Fear, Confusion* and *Emptiness.* In 2004 she was given the honor of Who's Who in Poetry and was nominated for poet of the year by Poetry.com. In her free time Melissa enjoys reading, writing and going out with her friends. She hopes to one day be on Broadway doing what she loves best, "singing."

Again

I can't believe it's happened again
I've fallen in love with my friend
He has a woman, he loves her so
yet I love him and he doesn't know.

Can't tell you why I'm livin' a lie
He just seems like the perfect guy
everything a girl could want and need
and some very special traits indeed.

Eyes so clear you can view the sea
Lips so full you could just die
A voice from the angels in heaven
And above all an exquisite gentleman.

I'll never know the touch of his hand
never know his love so true and grand
for to someone else he does belong
and for him I am left only to long.

Melissa Irene Oharriz

A. Owens

A Note from the Author

I was born in a small town in rural Mississippi, and very much consider myself a country girl. Although I've traveled, and lived in many places, the heart always leads me back home; where life is simple, quiet, and slow-paced and where the air is fresh and free from smog.

Brown Eyes

Brown eyes that watch me when I sleep,
Brown eyes that watch me when I speak.
Brown eyes that smile whenever I smile
Brown eyes that just want to stay awhile.

Brown eyes that love with an open heart,
Brown eyes that loved me from the start.
Brown eyes that've been through the hardest times
Brown eyes that have never lost their shine.

Brown eyes that know I'm always there,
Brown eyes that know I'll always care.
Brown eyes that know I'm not so tough,
Brown eyes that support me when the going gets rough.

Brown eyes with whom I spend my time
Brown eyes I want to be all mine
Brown eyes I adore come rain or shine,
Brown eyes I'll love till the end of time.

A. Owens

Charles P. Ries

Charles P. Ries lives in Milwaukee, Wisconsin. His narrative poems, short stories, interviews and poetry reviews have appeared in over one hundred print and electronic publications. He has received three Pushcart Prize nominations for his writing and most recently he read his poetry on National Public Radio's *Theme and Variations,* a program that is broadcast over seventy NPR affiliates. He is the author of THE FATHERS WE FIND, a novel based on memory. Ries is also the author of five books of poetry — the most recent entitled, *The Last Time* which was just released by The Moon Press in Tucson, Arizona. He is the poetry editor for Word Riot (www.wordriot.org) and he is on the board of the Woodland Pattern Bookstore in Milwaukee, Wisconsin. You may find additional samples of his work by going to: http://www.literarti.net/Ries/ and you may write him at charlesr@execpc.com

A citizen philosopher, Ries lived in London and North Africa after college where he studied the mystical teachings of Islam called Sufism. In 1989 he worked with the Dalai Lama on a program that brought American religious leaders and psychotherapists together for a weeklong dialogue. It was during this same week that the Dalai Lama was awarded

his Nobel Peace Prize. Ries has done extensive work with men's groups and worked with a Jungian Psychotherapist for over five years during which time he recorded five hundred dreams and learned to find the meanings in small things. He is a third degree Reiki healer, and has received advanced yoga training.

Ries has begun work on a second novel titled, SEEKER, which will follow his path as a mystic in Morocco, and subsequent floundering while living in Los Angeles. All of which has convinced him of the time-honored wisdom, "wherever you go, there you are" and "this isn't Kansas, Dorothy." He lives and writes in Milwaukee, Wisconsin, with his two daughters, four frogs, two cats, and one salamander on a wooded street along the lazy Menomonee River three doors down from his brother, Joe.

Fly, Fall Dreaming

Sometimes when my mind wanders, it feels like I am walking down a steep city street almost falling, as if I am flying and dreaming. In my dream a great wave cascades over my bald spot, as if it were an island in a sky blue Mediterranean Sea. Maybe dreams are like flying, falling.

I sit in the town square across from The Parroquia the great cathedral in San Miguel de Allende. It rises pink and brown in the early morning light. A woman dressed in white with a blood red shawl enters, making signs of the cross so quickly that I think she is swatting at flies or some invisible demon, but this is just her private ritual as she enters church. This is her crazy way of falling or dreaming. The arrangement we make in our mind with no one but ourselves.

I love the faces of the Indians. They are darker, more bronze in color than Spaniards. A young Indian girl walks toward me with the sun on her face. It is as if she is wearing a mask of polished copper. Her skin is radiant in the morning light, as she quickly passes by without looking at me. What is her dream?

Does she yearn to fall too? Are we alike in this way? San Miguel de Allende is a city built in the clouds on the shoulders of nine churches. The buildings are painted yellow, orange, red, green, and white, like great tropical birds. They stand against a clear blue sky. It is easy to fall here.

Time moves so slowly on this mountain of silver and dreaming. Two broad-bottomed house maids wearing uniforms the color of orange sherbet walk by. They carry a large green garbage container between them as they pass me in the early morning mist on their way to work. They are dreaming too. I can tell because their eyelids are closed, but their eyes are moving.

At dawn people pour buckets of water onto the cobblestone sidewalks outside their homes and shops. Sweeping them with brooms that look like witches riding sticks, they wash yesterday's debris away, yesterday's fallen dreams into the gutter. Sidewalks must be clean to carry dreamers.

Charles P. Ries

Holy Water

The following short story is an excerpted from my novel based on memory titled, THE FATHERS WE FIND: The Making of a Humble, Pleasant Boy.

Beyond the predictability of my father's work and prayer habits, there was one ritual he performed without fail. He blessed our beds. Each night after he'd washed and prayed, he'd come up to the two bedrooms on the second level of our home and make the sign of the cross over his children as they lay sleeping. Carrying a small glass bottle with a cross etched on the front, he sprinkled us with holy water. In his mind, he was showering us with a protective blanket of grace that would fill our room with angels and hover over us until morning. Most nights I was already fast asleep when he made his rounds, but on occasion just as sleep neared, I would feel a drop of holy water fall on my face or hand. It was a good feeling. An act of love that made the night safe; this rite of passage into the night was as sure as the sun rising in the morning. He'd silently come into the room I shared with my three brothers and bless our two beds. My father's world was built on routines and rituals. They kept his feet on the ground. They made the world a safe predictable place for him and for us. In these silent acts of kindness he extended his heart. These were the hugs and kisses he never shared with us. Through this twilight ritual he came as close to touching our souls as he ever would and ever did.

I'd go through the same routine every time I visited. I'd tell him I loved him and then sit in silence looking at him, waiting for him to say something. I wanted to run, but I owed it to him to stay there and say the words. He had earned at least that much respect. I repeated, "Dad, I love you," one final time and saw what I thought was a trickle of tears coming from his eyes as he sat hunched and strapped in his wheelchair, unable to talk, his body shaking uncontrollably. I wasn't sure if what I saw was the disease or a moment of real feeling. I had long given up on him, but still held out for a sign. I waited for the feelings buried deep within him to finally come out and breathe the same air with me.

As tears rolled down his cheeks I was certain I had finally *seen* him. I was certain that the curtain of his disease had parted for a moment and he was sharing something real with me. The view made me pity him all the more, but I could not reach down and find tears for him. I had stopped crying years ago. I would not weep for him now.

After a series of small strokes and following the administration of the Last Rites, he mercifully died. His eighty-eight year life was over. "*What am I to feel? How am I to be? It's my father, who just died.*" But I felt nothing. He had taught me well. I now had a firm grip on my feelings. They were stored a million miles away where they could do me no harm.

My father was not a warm and fuzzy kind of guy, my brother Joe began his eulogy. He wasn't a very playful person - he taught us how to work and all of my brothers and sisters know how to do that very well. I've learned some things are more important than being able to tell a good story or being able to entertain friends — things like integrity, sincerity, decency — in other words, faithfulness to one's beliefs.

I waited for something to open me up. For some sweet memory to find me and send me my tears, but nothing came. I was still angry with him; angry that I had to shut myself down; Angry that I couldn't remember him hugging or comprehending me. I had no connection with this man other than the holy water he sprinkled on my bed each night.

Every Tuesday night and often on Sunday, my dad would go to St. Vincent de Paul meetings and then would go out to visit and help families in need. My dad wasn't a do-gooder though because that implies superficiality. What he did, he did from his heart. He did what he did because of a deeply held belief that it was just the right thing to do.

As my brother continued, I stopped listening. I withdrew and looked forward to the after burial luncheon and drinking a few Brandy Old Fashions to my old man, the best minker that ever lived.

With closed eyes, I reached back and searched for my memories. The meaning of who I had become would be discovered by carefully remembering these building blocks of my nature.

A series of snap shots, smells, colors and dreams passed before me - the mysterious pieces of a boy on verge of becoming. Splashing in a puddle created by a late August storm with my younger brother. Feeling the close quarters of my dad's 1949 Buick as the nine of us crowd together enroute to my Uncle's for Easter Sunday dinner. Abducting my aunt's poppy seed tort from the desert table and carrying it into a near by clothes closet so I could have all its creamy goodness to myself and then crying hysterically as my mother discovered me and liberated my friend from my intoxicated fingers.

Snap shots. Fragments of memory…

Green farm fields. The chirping of my father's mink after weaning and the smell of pelting season. Snow forts, ice-skating in the swamp and my mother's garden with its raspberries, strawberries, rhubarb and vegetables. The smell of bread baking in the kitchen. A world of constancy nestled in the heart of Wisconsin.

Our red brick house that stood next to my grandparent's cream brick home. And next to our home my uncle's and just thirty feet further south my aunt's. We'd laughed and called it Riesville. Four homes along a black top country road populated with seventeen children and eight adults. The only things that ever changed were the weather, the seasons and our ages.

It felt as if we had always been here. My ancestors homesteaded this land 1810. Fresh off boat from Austria, my great-great grandfather bought his stake in America. Two more generations of dairy farmers followed and then came my father who would raise mink rather then dairy cattle. Hard working, church going, frugal men and women who made good use of their time on earth…

The earliest days of my life were without surprise or pain. There was nothing to distinguish one day from the other. Until my eyes started to open and as natural as life itself, I began to see. And the life I remember began.

"Chucky, is the mail truck here yet?" my mother called from the kitchen.

"Not yet. I'm watching," I called back. My nose pressed against the window that looked north toward my grandparent's house. Their home, and Riesville's large postal box, stood beneath an Oak Tree whose branches reached like protecting arms over the sky blue roof and soft yellow brick exterior of their house.

"Well, it'll be here in a minute or two," she replied.

I was old enough for my first chore. At four years old I was big enough to find a place in the factory of my father's farm.

"I can see it! I see the mail truck," I shouted as I raced through the kitchen and out the back door, running with short urgent strides. Propelling myself along a foot worn path that carried me and a procession of mail collectors before me through a sparse orchard of crab apple trees toward the mailbox into which all of the mail destined for Riesville was placed.

"You must be the new delivery boy?" a voice called to me from the mail truck.

"Yes sir. It's my job."

"Think you can carry all this stuff? You're just a little guy," I heard the voice say as a tanned arm reached out of the side window and placed the day's news, bills and letters into my out stretched arms.

It was the commencement of my working life. It was the day I became a little man.

"Well look who's here," I heard my grandmother Mary say as I opened the screen door leading to her kitchen. "So, you're in charge now, huh?" she said in her thick German accent.

"I'm in charge of mail," I replied, holding the overflow bundle. Hugging it and making sure not one item escaped my embrace.

"I see that. Well you just put the mail there on the table and sit down," she said pointing to the chair where she wanted her grandson to sit. "You look hungry. You have three more houses to go before lunchtime. You need some apple pie," she said in a way that always sounded like an order.

"Grandma, I have mail to deliver now," I tried to explain, letting her know I knew my job.

"You will. But first you get some pie. You work. You eat. Little men have to eat," she said placing a wedge of pie in front of me from one of the four she'd set on the table to cool. It was my diploma to manhood – a quarter-pan-man-sized certificate of achievement. As I sat and took a fork full of the warm treat, I realized I wouldn't complete my route until I'd finished her pie. As I ate, she talked to me in her short matter-of-fact sentences. "God gave us a good day. A good day for picking raspberries and canning tomatoes," she said as she sorted the mail, not looking up until she had placed the day's delivery onto four neat piles. She tied each pile with a piece of butcher's twine and then took a long admiring look at the young man sitting at her table and nodded affirmatively, mentally noting that he was right on track to becoming a good, productive little Ries. Her gift of pie was God smiling on my life.

As I neared the end of my sweet tribute the phone rang, "Yes, Chucky's here. Sure, he'll have plenty of room for lunch. He's busy with grandma now. We're talking. We have business to do. He'll be home soon. He has mail to deliver," she said to my mother who'd called wondering where the new mail carrier had disappeared. With my plate now spotless, I got up and received an uncharacteristic hug from my grandmother and resumed my route. She'd laid the three bundles of mail in my arms, "you get moving now. Your mom's got your lunch waiting. Scoot."

I bounded out of the kitchen and saw my grandfather Peter coming up the gravel road that lead to the carpenter-shop, "better get moving Chucky, everyone's wondering if the mailman thought you were a letter and mailed you to Green Bay."

"Okay grandpa, I'm moving now. Grandma had pie for me."

"I'm sure of that," he said as he watched me make my way back along the path, through orchard and over a wide mowed field where we played softball.

I walked the final hundred yards to the far end of Riesville where I delivered my aunt's and then my uncle's mail. Knocking on each door, handing the bundle through the opening to a, "thanks Chucky; you want to stay for lunch."

"Nope. I had pie at grandma's. Now I have to get home for lunch," I said as I sped back across the softball field and entered the kitchen where my six siblings were already half way through with their meal.

"All done?" my mother asked.

"Yup, done for this day."

Well, take a seat and have some lunch or did Grandma fill you full of pie?" she said, seeing the telltale sign of early desert on the corners of my mouth and clinging to the front of my shirt.

It was my first day of work and my life's first memory.

Charles P. Ries

Jason Schramm

My name is Jason Schramm, although I plan to write professionally under the penname J. Michaels. I am a husband to my wife Lisa and a father of two. My oldest child is Jacob (6) and the youngest is his little sister Alyssa (2) whom we call Issa. We currently reside in one of the many suburbs of Chicago near the area that my wife and I grew up. I have been writing poetry since an early age, and I have written hundreds of poems to date. Currently I am working on my first novel that I hope to have published by the end of this year. The working title is, "*Abandoned.*" I hope that you will all look for it when it becomes available in stores. A great friend of mine was fond of saying, "Yesterday is the past, tomorrow is the future, today is a gift, and that is why we call it the present." For me, those words sum up a way of life. They are truly words to live by. Love life, and live with love, until we meet again.

Jacob the Brave

Jacob's sleeping sound at night
When he wakes with such a fright
Something stirring out of sight
It's a bear!
It's a bear!

Jacob's shaking full of fear
Wonder what is moving there
What is causing such a scare?
It's a bear!
It's a bear!
The shadow looms high on the wall
Arms outstretched with two great paws
Jacob wonders whom to call
It's a bear!
It's a bear!
Mom and Dad are sound in bed
What if the bear comes over instead?
I hope that bear has been well-fed
It's a bear!
It's a bear!
The fear is strong this is true
But Jacob's brave through and through
He'll hit the lights that's what he'll do
It's a bear!
It's a bear!
The lights will give him such a scare
That he'll go running far from here
And tell all the other bears, beware!
Jacob's there!
Jacob's there!
Out of bed he hopped right quick
Ran to the switch and with a flick
What the lights showed, made him sick
It's a bear?
It's a bear?

A little girl stood in the corner
Issa Bear's what Daddy calls her
Alyssa is Jacob's baby sister
Issa Bear
Issa Bear
So what's this story really taught us?
Things look different in the darkness
And little sisters can be a menace!
Issa Bear
Issa Bear

JASON SCHRAMM

Miryam Shields

Myriam Alford Shields was born in Bogotá, Colombia in 1935. She studied art, literature and design. Mrs. Shields dedicates time to designing a line of clothes for children. Mrs. Shields also has illustrated and written several story books for children. Myriam married when she was 23 years old and had three children: Michael, Lisa and Jay. Jay the youngest of the three siblings turned 20 years in 1988, when the family suffered his loss. The tragedy of their lives began for always when their dear Jay died. Myriam Shields' poems are dedicated to her Jay. The love and kindness touched all of those who knew him. Jay is the inspiration for Myriam's poems, stories and paintings.

http://www.lovepetalsjay.com/JAYPLACE.html Celebrando una vida…

"La medida del amor, es amor sin medida."

http://www.angelfire.com/de/lovepetals/poems.html

Celebrating a life…

"The measurement of the love is love in an unrestrained fashion."

Sun Set

Brilliant colors in the sky
Against the blue ocean waves
Foam gathers at the shoreline
I stand and wait…my love my Jay
Your spirit bright as the colors of the sky
I feel your touch as the breeze goes by
Tender and soft you pass me by
Your scent I breathe I close my eyes
My darling my son I love you so…….
In solitude I await by the shoreline
You come to me in waves of light
Then………..
You are here by my side.

Myriam Alford Shields

Adrian Spendlow

Adrian Spendlow, poet is a full time performer, working on stage [with music or without] and in the community. National (UK) tours include a specialty in shows for the visually impaired. Drama poems for children reach the small child within us all and a writer's guide for children will be in the hands of the publisher by the end of the year.

Amber Eyes

Delayed shock
Pulsing on empty
Two glasses and glowing
It is love
Unrequited
And even *not happening*
She's young and she's gone
And her eyes
And my god!
Ambery golden
Deep and clear
If there is any justice
She'll walk in here now
It is meant
Or why feel like this
Just because it's impossible
Doesn't mean it's not fate
We were destined
She meant it
She said that
She looked in my eyes
Was so glad for
One last meet
So wanted to hold me
And I wish it
I wish it right now
If true love is internal
She will walk in here now
Bodies not important
I fancied but lose detail
It was eyes and person
It *is* the feeling;
The knowing
We know
From the moment
What moment, you ask me

The one that is crystal;
When I wake in the night
I wake in the night
And I see her looking at me
And no matter how I doubt
It comes out that it was then
If there is,
Any chance for me
She will walk in at this moment
She *is* here
I haven't noticed
There she is
Breezing in now
Knowing that *the* moment
Was forever and for us
Even if forever isn't credence
Or believed in
Bitter from break up
I disbelieve in forever
In exclusive
In the true love
There she is
In she comes now
Close to my eye
Like the dream that keeps happening
There she is
I will wait here
No I'll walk now
It is kismet
Fate says,
We will meet up
Fate
Fate
Fate
Fate

ADRIAN SPENDLOW

A Song

So bitter
So brittle
So lost
Within her own world
I cannot really be
With this girl
There are battles lost
She's lost within
I never ever never can surpass
I cannot really reach; this lass
She gets dragged back
And bitter hits
Tears me to bits
It's tragic
Backs up on our consciousness
Our senses
This is always

I will always always
Miss these days

Adrian Spendlow

Linda Stypulkowski

Linda Barroso Stypulkowski was born in New Jersey. She began to write early in life, growing up in a little town called Garwood, where the people who knew her, and loved her, encouraged her to continue to write her short stories and poems.

Being raised by an Italian Mother, and having a Portuguese Father, Linda also began to master the art of cooking early in life, and Linda is now a State Certified Culinary Instructor and home chef. Combining her passion for life and her life experiences, she takes great pride in her culinary teaching as well as her writings. Married and the mother of two grown children, Linda is currently writing her first book.

A Favorite Christmas Eve

I have to admit as I continue to grow older, that most of my recollections of holidays past, over time, are beginning to run one year into the other. And, after years have gone by, I am grateful to pictures of children in pajamas, posing near a Christmas tree, and happy to see the date and the year on the bottom right hand corner of my family video recordings. I call them memory aids. Cherished moments in time that would become blurred and probably disappear forever were it not for the physical evidence that it had once existed at all. Maybe that is why, what you do remember, is so very special and hopefully happy.

I asked my children recently what Christmas they remembered as being really special in their young adult lives so far. I listened as they described to me their memories of that evening some years ago, and I was secretly overjoyed to know that what they considered to be one of the "best", was also my favorite too. I smiled when I thought back to that Christmas Eve, not so long ago. For what they did not know was that I knew why it had been so great. I knew this because it had been my Christmas present that in the end helped to make their Christmas Eve so joyful too.

Jill and Richard were small.....I cannot remember exactly how old which one was, nor even the year that it was. I only know that they were both so excited that Santa was coming that evening. But on that day, that Christmas Eve Day, my husband and I packed up our car, bundled up the children, and drove to my parents' home in the very early afternoon. My parents were getting up there in age, and I wanted to help them get ready for our family Christmas Eve celebration that would take place later that evening. It was going to be a hard, long day. There was so much more to do, and so little time left.

All afternoon my husband and father took care of the children, playing and occupying them both, trying to keep them out of the busy kitchen where my mother and I worked, side by side, cleaning and cooking for our traditional Italian Christmas Eve dinner. Somewhere in late afternoon, my father came into the kitchen and whispered into my ear, "I have a big surprise for you later."

"What?" I asked.

"Never mind," he said. "You'll see later," and disappeared from the kitchen.

I tried to get my mother to tell me what the surprise was, but forget it. She would not budge. It was going to be my surprise from my father, and it would have to wait until later.

Christmas Eve began. Somehow between dinner and dessert, the company, the laughter and the presents, I had forgotten what my father had told me. But, when everyone was busy and talking among each other, my father called me into the kitchen.

"Get the children dressed warm, and meet me in the garage," he said.

Without a moment's hesitation I did as I was told and we all piled into the car. My father, my children and I drove off. No one else, no other, no spouse, no sister, no aunts or uncles, just us, alone went in the car driving away for that special ride.

I can still remember when he backed the car out from the garage onto the street. I do not remember what I said, but what I saw took my breath away. For, what took a second or two for my eyes to recognize was that our entire block was lit up in candles. There were candles everywhere. Home upon home, row upon row, little white candlelight's flickering in the moonlight, in white paper bags filled with sand.

The candles lit up every front porch and driveway as far as the eye could see. In that small little town, with snow still on the ground, and with help from the stars and the moonlight, those candles, in their little white bags, made up a beautiful sight to behold. And then my father began to drive the car, ever so slowly, up and down the streets, as we all absorbed the beauty and quiet of the night. Not a word was said between us as he drove, but I remember the children were in awe, their little eyes wide with delight. For there was such magic in something as simple as those candles glowing and flickering on that cold Christmas Eve night. Then, as if it could not get any better than this, the bell chimes from the church tower, in the center of town, began to play. Their chimes rung out throughout the town, and on that silent night, "Silent Night" could be heard playing. I knew then that it was probably going to be one of the best and most beautiful Christmas Eves I would ever have in my life.

We were not gone very long, maybe only a half hour, but before we returned home, I looked at my father and thanked him. "Thank you, Daddy. What a wonderful surprise." And in his simple, yet loving way, he smiled, took my hand and kissed it. "I knew you would love it," was all he said.

Later that evening I found out that the town had held a fund drive to raise money for a worthy cause. The fire department organized the fund drive by selling the candles, the bags and sand for a minimal cost, and what started out as a fund drive became a town project where everyone participated, and then begun to anticipate the lighting of the candles on Christmas Eve.

There have been many more Christmas Eves since that one. Times changes and life does go on. Children get older. Grandchildren grow up. The beauty of that Christmas Eve was the simplicity of the gift. Just a simple gift from a father to a daughter; Just a father and a daughter and moment between them in a lifetime.

That Day in July

The street on West End Avenue was quiet and still that beautiful summer day so very long ago. I can still remember waking up to the smell of the summer breeze blowing in from our bedroom window, above our heads, warm and so sweet, where my twin sister, Sandra, and I slept together in our twin beds. The birds were singing too that morning, loud and long, and if anyone was happy, it surly was me; for summertime was in full bloom, and it was going to be another hot and glorious day. After all, it was July, in northeast New Jersey, and the sun came to this month as surely as the snow would come in January. A childhood filled with joy, and the happiness that another great day was beginning, in the life of an eight year old little girl living in Old Bridge, New Jersey.

As happy as I was, I still had a hard time understanding why Sandra was confined to bed. My mother and father had said that Sandra was suffering from an illness that I could not comprehend, but did come to try to understand that bed rest was the only way for her to heal. A condition in the early part of the century known as "rheumatic fever; " a slow, steady, murmur of the heart, which had so many other related conditions attached to it, causing my twin to be put to bed for the next nine months. It was strange to not be able to have my twin sister to run with and play with outside in the woods, across the street from where we lived. I missed her more than words could possibly say, and I knew that she was hurting badly ....missing out on summer, and not being able to go anywhere or be with me and our small gathering of friends. But she was getting better, and most of my day was still spent with her.

That morning, in the bedroom, by her bedside, we were reading and playing Color Forms. After a few hours of sticking small plastic colored pieces of plastic onto a black stenciled outline, we switched to playing gin rummy, where Sandra was an expert at beating me. She beat me again that morning. "See Nona, I can really play this game" she said, and I replied "I know, and good thing that we love it so." And then it happened, that moment in time that never goes away, and stayed with me all these years ....the doorbell rang, and I yelled to Mommy "I'll get it."

As I opened the door, with my mother standing in back of me, there stood four of my brother's teenage friends. They were dressed in black T-shirts, with long side burns and cigarettes dangling from their mouths. "Good morning Mrs. Barroso! It's a beautiful day here in Old Bridge! It's David, my 16 year old teen age brother, Tony's, best friend. "It sure is," my mother said as she welcomed them into our living room. How cool they must have felt to be so young, and so free.

"We need Tony's help in moving a piano. Can Tony come with us to work a small delivery job?" David asked. "I don't know. He's sleeping." my mother says. "I'll get him," I say, and then immediately yelled at our dog Buddy to "Go get brother!" Fast as a flash, Buddy, our brown and white mixed six year old mutt took to the upstairs, two and three steps at a time, and racing up those steps to get my brother. After a minute or two, I expected to see my brother come bouncing down those steps, but nothing happened. No brother. No Buddy. So, I wondered where they both could be, and realized that I had to go climb up those steps to see what was happening, I ran upstairs, and turning into my brother's bedroom, there, lying on my brother's bed, eyes closed and enjoying his rest, lay Buddy. Together the two of them were snuggled together, close and inseparable, sleeping.

"Brother, get up. David and the guys are here," I said. "What?????" he replied, slowly opening his eyes for the first time that morning, yet rolling over fast to avoid the direct sun light shining into his eyes. "Get up, brother! I yelled, Mommy says to get you up ....the guys are here and they need you for a summer job." "Okay, I'll be right there," he replied. And so I walked out of his room, and came down the stairs, ready to tell all the guys and my mother that he had rolled over and went back to sleep. But, to my utter amazement, he came bouncing down those same steps wearing old jeans, but a clean white T-shirt, his face unwashed, eyes still sleepy and a little grumpy. He kissed my mother good-bye and walked out the door. Not a word was said, and little did we know that we would never see him again.

When they left, I went back to the bedroom with Sandra, and sat on the bed. Soon my mother came into the room with a large tray of tuna sandwiches and fruit, and we had this wonderful time laughing and talking and eating ....all of us together, that Monday early afternoon. After we finished lunch, I gathered all of the dirty dishes and glasses, and made it a point to do the dishes and help my Mother clean up the kitchen. "Stay and play with Sandra" I said to her, I'll do the dishes. I can still see myself at the kitchen sink, washing the dishes and rinsing all of the soap off the glasses when the wall phone rang.

"Hello?" I said, as I answered the phone, and who should be on the phone but my brother's girlfriend, Arlene. Sobbing and screaming into my ear, she cried "Get your mother." I could hear her anguish, and my very first thought was to wonder, Oh Boy! What could he have done now? And then I thought that maybe he was in jail for drinking and driving because of an incident that recently happened where he had come home drunk. So alarmed and knowing that I had to get my mother immediately, I dropped the phone and ran into the bedroom. "Mommy, Arlene is on the phone and needs you right away," I cried.

My mother jumped off the bed, and following her, ran into the kitchen to pick up the phone. I can still see her as she put the phone to her ear and says to

Arlene "What's the matter honey?", and then I hear her scream a blood curling scream that I could never, ever forget, as she falls to the floor in a faint. I then picked up the phone and yelled to Arlene, "What's the matter?", and Arlene screamed back to me, "Your brother is dead."

At that same horrible moment, my mother wakes and screams "Go wake up Daddy." So I ran upstairs to our bedroom, where my father is sleeping, after working nights, so that my mother could take care of my sister in their master bedroom during the day. "Daddy, Daddy, get up! Something has happened to brother," I cried. My father jumped out of bed and grabbed his pants ....his work uniform from Ballentine Beer Company, with the change jingling in his pockets, I saw him trying to walk and put on his pants at the same time, as he somehow manages to make it down the steps, and turn into the kitchen where my mother has just hung up the phone and is crouching over the counter, crying and sobbing ....''Tony's dead" she screams to him, as he runs to her and holds her tightly, and then the both of them are crying and sobbing. I am beyond upset ....afraid and so scared and worried. I kept thinking that this must be a nightmare, and somehow they have it all wrong. He couldn't possibly be dead ...not brother. And then I heard Sandra, screaming from the bedroom ....''Nona, Nona ....what is wrong?" And I ran into the bedroom, and crying, told her the news. "Brother's been killed." Knowing no details, and not knowing what else to say, we both cried and I wonder what really happened, and is my brother coming back home alive.

Within minutes the house was filled with people from all over the township. The fire department is out front, the policemen are in the house, trying to comfort my mother. The neighbors, her girlfriends, and even the family doctor were there. Somehow, within a matter of five minutes of receiving the phone call from Arlene, the entire town is finding out that my brother has been killed, and everyone is coming to the house to offer their condolences and comfort to my mother and father. And I am standing by myself, alone, in the living room watching this horrible, painful scene taking place. They've all forgotten about me. The crying and the screaming, the sobbing and the tears .....And poor Sandra is all alone in the bedroom, crying into her pillow. I try to spend a few minutes with her, but there were so many people in the house, and I had to find out what really happened. I was in a state of denial. He can't be dead ...he can't be.

Just as I walked into the living room there was a police man standing in the middle of the room, looking at me, with tears in his eyes, and a look of such sorrow. He walked up to me and puts his arm around my shoulder, but says not a word. I turn and look at him, and grabbing his hand, I ask him "Are you sure? Could you have made a mistake? Is my brother really dead?" And he replies, "Yes, sweetheart ....there is no mistake." And with that, I walked away, into the hallway and into the family room where my mother is half on the couch and half on the floor sobbing and crying. Her girlfriends are by her side, trying to pick her up and put her up on the couch, but it's no use. The grief is beyond words.

Next I saw our family physician, Dr. Cryin, come into the room, and he was giving her a needle. I'm wondering why he is giving my mother a needle, when one of my mother's girlfriends grabs me and picks me up in her arms, and holds me tightly to her, hugging me and kissing me. "Don't worry honey, she'll be ok. The doctor is tying to give her something that will keep her calm right now." And then, as if it could not get any worse, my mother is crying and sobbing and holding onto my father and at the same time, she is changing her house dress and putting on a new, clean house dress from the closet in the family room. I realize that by her changing her dress, she is going somewhere, and I wonder where she could be off too.

Coming to me and kissing me and holding me, my mother tells me "I'm going to the home of the boys that were responsible for driving the truck and moving the piano." She says, "What happened, Mommy, you didn't tell me," I say. With a look of such pain and such agony, she then begins to tell me the whole story, and gives me all of the facts that up until this point were unknown to me.

"Brother and the boys were helping to deliver an upright piano, as a summer job. When they got to the house to pick up the piano, for the delivery, brother sat at the back of the truck, because there was no room in the front of the truck. And they had to go around the roundabout, but they didn't realize that the piano was on rollers, and as they went around the circle, in town, the piano rolled, and fell on brother, pushing him off the truck and crushing him to death."

He's dead. There's no denial now ....I'll never see him again. And that summer day, I learned the true meaning of a broken heart that day, and if I thought that I had many more years of childhood left, I was sadly mistaken. For in that split second or two, my whole life changed, including the mother and father I once knew. Life would never, ever be the same again, and I knew it even then.

LINDA STYPULKOWSKI

Idania Temiño

Idania Figueroa Temiño was born in Cuba. She moved to Miami, Florida in 1968. In 2003 published a poetry book in Spanish "Poesia sencillamente profunda." Mothered three daughters and recently had a grandchild named Madison. Writing plays an important role in her life, her way to express unspoken words.

I'll Wait

Friendship, is your silence
Loneliness, your home
It is the way you express your feelings,
When a problem is unsolved
But I'd like you to know
That I'll always be close to you
Even when there is little to say,
Or when you lock yourself up in your world,
I will not be bothered
I will just sit at your door
Waiting for you

Idania Figueroa Temiño

Until the Day You Came

Seeking for an answer,
I found many questions
Searching for a light
I walked through my shadows
Reaching for the highest
I climbed many ladders
Until the day you came
To rescue my soul

IDANIA FIGUEROA TEMIÑO

Linda Turner-Zwetkov

Linda Turner-Zwetkov is an American living in Austria since 1980. She has a husband, a 14-year-old son, and four dogs. For 30 years Linda was involved as a full-time Christian volunteer working in seven countries. The experiences she gained in such work were the fuel that ignited her ambition to write. Storytelling has always been Linda's thing, and when she saw how much these stories helped people, she got serious about writing them down. Linda is the co-founder and president of "Children's Bridge of Hope," a non-profit society dedicated to rescuing abandoned babies in Romania. (www.childrens-bridgeofhope.org)

Benny the Teacher

I have a little dog, a Chihuahua, named Benny. I've learned a lot from him. Yes, he's not just a dog, he's a teacher of the highest caliber. When I come home, he greets me with such joy, such wild enthusiasm that I'm afraid he'll have a heart-attack. When my husband comes home, even if it's two minutes later, he repeats the whole thing. We jokingly call him our "reception committee" or "fan club." All dogs do this, but Benny has modified it. How? Well, each greeting is crowned with Benny's "offering": a raggedy, orange and black toy tiger held captive between little white teeth.

When I wake up in the morning, with my first yawn, a little brown eye pops open. If I stretch, I see a little tail start to wagging sideways. When I finally manage to sit up, Benny's morning routine goes into effect. He stretches, yawns, drags his tummy across the carpet and with a Herculean hop, he's on the bed, tiger in tow. The day has begun.

Whatever happy occasion may occur, whether it be getting ready to go out or anticipating dinner, Benny always comes to you with his tiger. For months we couldn't figure it out. "What's with this tiger? Why does he always bring this thing?" It wasn't clear till we really seriously thought it over. Then it dawned on us, "He has nothing else to offer us." And so that's his little way of saying, "Here, you can have my favorite toy." It's an "offering" so to speak, a trade. And as soon as he gets the tummy rub or a doggie munchie, or the leash comes out, he drops the tiger and is in 7th heaven.

So, I was thinking how all of us are like Benny. We can only offer to God what he has already given us, but the difference, the thing that makes the sacrifice desireable to Him, is not the size of the gift, but the way that we bring it. Do we bring it with joy and thankfulness? Do we bring it with humility; appreciation? Do we bring it with faith? So, I learned after 3 years that it's not "what" it's "how". Yes, Benny has taught me a lot.

LINDA TURNER-ZWETKOV

Ten Once Again

Speeding down the hill, heart sinking
on my bike of metal clinking
like medieval armor chinking,
"I'm fifty five! What was I thinking??"

Too late now; I swallow hard
while sending up a prayer to God
and speeding down the steeping hill
Undaunted, terrified and thrilled.

Rattling chains and handle-bars
"God, please don't let me hit a car!
Or hit a stone!" Oh, ignominious death!
"So irresponsible" I hold my breath

With thoughts as seconds racing by
Bouncing tires and watering eyes
The wind whips up and on it's wings
Exalted I, my laughter sings

I'm 55? No! Only 10!
And racing down that hill again!

LINDA TURNER-ZWETKOV

Twixt!

(Enter Shakespearean hero with a flourish...)

The music swells, I feel the prose!
So pardon me while I take this rose
And clench it firm betwixt my teeth
For such a bud shall grace no wreath!

We'll dance the tango o'er the Nile
a la "Casa Blanca" style!
And when ecstatic numbers done
We'll do the twist like we did last sum....mer.

Oh, feelings come and feelings go!
Let's live it up! Just let her blow!
Get it out and get it off
Who cares how loud they shout or scoff?
Why question why I question "why"?
Why should I walk when I can fly!
Why drive when you could take a bus?
I'll end this now with one word. Thus

Linda Turner-Zwetkov

Kathleen Vasilas

Kathy Vasilas was born on November 25, 1966 in Chicago, Illinois. She spent most of her life in the same city where she was born. There she met the love of her life, Steve.

Kathy and Steve started dating in 1986. Steve suffered from an accident in 1988. Before, during and after the accident they shared their love. True love conquers all because they were married on September 6, 1998. To this date, both Kathy and Steve love respect and cherish each other.

They moved to Miami, Florida in 1998. Steve is very active and works for The Miami Project to Cure Paralysis. Kathy is the owner of Head to Toe Salon and Beauty Spa in Miami, Florida.

Dear Journal

Years ago, my husband Steve and I had a bright future ahead of us. We lived in Chicago with good paying jobs and lots of friends and family around us. We were so young and so in love that we never considered anything but positive things could lie in our future.

Then one fateful night a careless driver forced Steve off the road on an isolated highway. His vehicle traveled so far from the road. Nobody noticed the wreckage until the light of the following day.

Fortunately, my husband was spared that evening. But only barely, and I thank God everyday that he is here with me. Unfortunately, Steve has never had the use of his legs since the accident. Needless to say our lives changed very much since then.

Steve was offered an amazing opportunity to be involved with exciting new research in the field of curing paralysis. The opportunity to work toward a cure and help so many others with similar afflictions was a dream come true. However, we would have to move to Miami, Florida and away from all of our loved ones in order to pursue that dream.

The most difficult day since the accident, was the day I looked into my dearest mother, sister and brothers. I had to tell them I was leaving my home. We came to Florida without knowing many people. Nevertheless, we quickly made friends and both of us leapt into work head first. Steve has made amazing strides with The Miami Project and I am very happy with my beauty salon.

Not everything has been perfect since we've moved here. During the most recent hurricane season our home suffered water damage from flooding. We were also recently robbed of many of our prize possessions. The insurance company has been unwilling to offer anything near full value without receipts for family heirlooms that were purchased decades ago.

These hardships are minor compared to the difficulties that our dear friends and colleagues of my husband are faced with on a daily basis. There are such amazingly strong people that keep pushing on against the most difficult odds. I also see the effort Steve puts into his work everyday and I am left with awe.

My husband struggles through some of lives' most mundane activities. Yet, he has still has the energy to put a recently paralyzed patient at ease about the future. I love my husband with all of my heart and I want to do for him what he does for so many others. I want to make him a little bit more comfortable in the midst of a difficult situation.

Kathy Vasilas

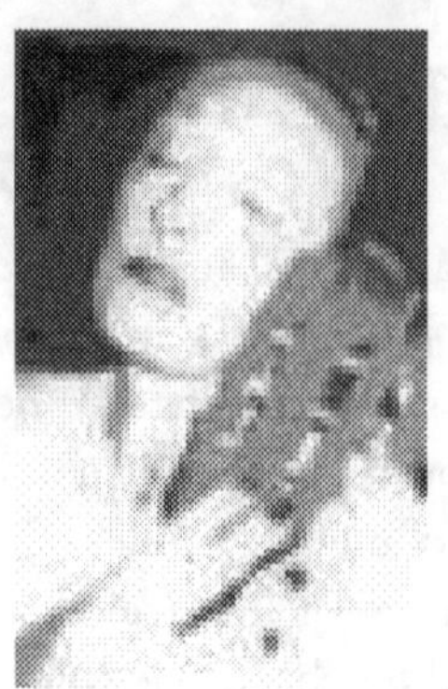

Sand-dee Rose Waybill

A Note from the Author

I was born in England during April 1966, and immigrated to Australia in the late 1980's, where I currently reside in Wollongong. I have written poetry since my youth, but had not submitted any for publication until the last decade. After my second entry to a contest at Poetry.com won an editor's choice award in 2004 I began to receive requests for further poetry without having to bother to search for publishing opportunities. I tend to write in three various styles, (spiritual explanations, everyday verse, and descriptive words.) Samples can be located at poetry.com.

Commencing in 2005 I have taken up writing other than poetry, and am currently ¼ through writing a biography which explains my spiritual philosophy, & am also researching publishers and conducting e-mail interviews for a book about the music scene in current day San Francisco. I have ideas for a science fiction novel and a drama set in England waiting to be written too, with perhaps a poetry book to follow after. For a sample of my non-poetical works please read my web-journal located @ my personal website, www.nashvilletubes.bravepages.com, where you can also find information on my continuing work.

The Fruit Bowl

A withered red apple sits unpicked to one side,
The fruit around it tries to let it hide,
No-one really wants to eat it, so
To a destiny of pie-fill it will need to go!
A solid obese pear sits below the downy peach,
Yet to none of these fruits will my fingers reach.
Shiny cherries scattered everywhere like the first snow,
Gleaming, juicy and delicious, is where my fingers go!

SAND-DEE ROSE WAYBILL

The Mask of Convention

If you look for love, but see romance and situation,
If you look for marriage, but see ceremony and certificate,
If you look for success, but see
College, career, status, and cash,
You are looking through the mask of convention,
And seeing 21st century life as you are told to live it

If you look for love, and see caring, sharing spirits,
If you look for marriage, and see soul-union and affection,
If you look for success, and see family,
Peace, wisdom, and nature,
You are looking through the mask of truth,
And seeing life as it really should be lived

Sand-Dee Rose Waybill

Melissa-Marie Zirini

Melissa-Marie Zirini received her Masters of Arts at the University of Denver's Graduate School of International Studies, in International Studies. She attended the University of Central Florida and attained her Bachelor of Arts in International Relations.

Melissa-Marie has enjoyed writing stories and poetry since childhood. It has been her one true passion and favorite pass time. She enjoys reading and researching Medieval Literature and World Mythology. In the future, she hopes to share her vast imagination with the world by publishing her own novel. You can contact Melissa-Marie by email: mzirini@hotmail.com

The Journey

Keep a dream in your heart
With hopes and goals raised high
With a smile and gleam you start
Remembering a loud scream can mean less than a gentle sigh
Enjoy the day as it comes your way
Take in every moment as an intoxicating wine
The sun and moon shine their mystical magic on your head
Strive forward! Nothing can stop you unless you let it enter your soul
The demons and monsters of failure and ignorance
Are defeated by the gallant knights of hope and perseverance
The wisdom of a sage; the knowledge of the scholar
It does not come from books; the answer lies around you
Within a grain of sand, a burning flame, a gentle breeze
The answer lies within you
If your goal rests beyond the river
Do not forget the ride on the boat
If your goal rests on the mountain top
Do not forget the climb
Has it taken you a lifetime? Or has it taken you a day?
If you answered the latter, then you best start again

MELISSA-MARIE ZIRINI

On a Scottish Moor

I knew him once before, I did
A hundred years or more
A noble lord of Russian past
On a Scottish moor

His eyes were fixed and stern and bold
A gallant knight was he
His manner strict and strong and cold
But naught but gentle when with me

The castle hung above the sea
That water's siren call softly echoing
And I, I was young, young and free
And I was happy by the sea

To the west the highlands lay
The land I knew a 'fore
The land of immortals the old ones say
Holding more truth than lore

Immortality has a price
A price it holds quite high
Eternity for life
A life in which you die

There are few who have this gift
Or curse if you are wise
My love and I are of that kind
Our life is but a lie

But death doth come to us
As tragic and cruel as it may be
For our own kind must be the judge
Of who should lose their immortality

But I have a tale to tell
I left it for the while
Now again—my love, ah yes,
How he made me smile

The years swept by
The moor turned gray
And the waves crashed louder each day
And my love, he could no longer stay

The mermaid's tears flowed from her eyes
As free as rivers run
And her cries cut through the night
Until the break of the sun

I know that mermaid well
I hear her every night
She waits for her love, too
Patiently, for any sight

And so I sit and wait for him
Through rain and through wind
I wait for him by the shore
I wait for him on a Scottish moor

Melissa-Marie Zirini

Future

Andrei Alessandri

Andrei Alessandri is a teenager. He was born in Miami, Florida on March 30, 1991. His mother Erika Pflucker was born in Lima, Peru and his father in Buenos Aires, Argentina. He speaks Spanish fluently. Andrei attended eighth grade in Buenos Aires., Argentina. He is currently enrolled in Coral Gables Senior High School located in Florida, U.S.A. In his spare time he enjoys reading mystery novels, writing poetry, playing his guitar. As for sports he likes to play tennis.

Love and Hate

’Tis to love
’tis to hate
’tis like a dove
’tis but a snake
It loves and wishes
It growls and hisses.
Tis like a speech all well and thought
And yet like a child not yet taught.

Andrei Alessandri

Young Man

You think your life is coming apart
And you only have shards of a broken heart.
You think your life is full of hate
And you think you just can't wait.
But try to do the best you can
And hold the butterfly softly in your hand.
Live life for what is worth
And cherish your time on this earth.
Do as you will and can
And guess what boy; now you're a man!

ANDREI ALESSANDRI

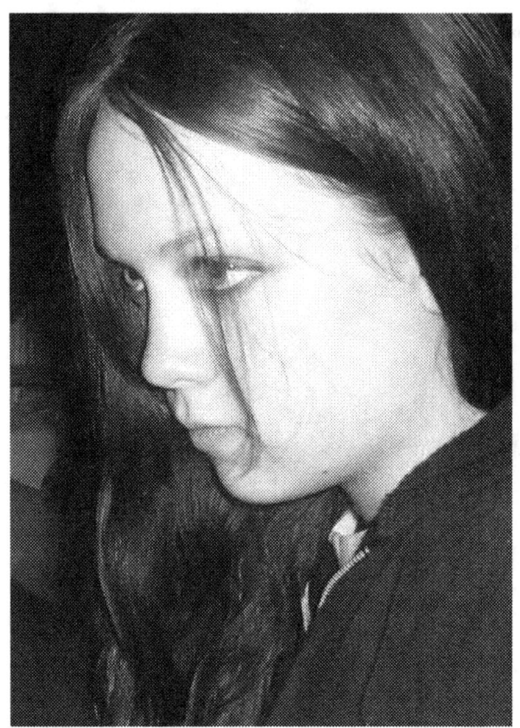

Kristin Aughenbaugh

Kristin Aughenbaugh is a 15 year old high school student from "Middle of a Cornfield" Illinois. She is a huge fan of wide varieties of music and art and hopes to one day attend art school. In her spare time she enjoys video gaming, reading, writing, drawing, and photography.

Porcelain

I want you
stranger in my eyes
take my heart and all its lies
touch the glass on this cold night
the forsaken shall fall
into this empty void that is my heart
touch it
ashes become shards
but I need you to
bring me back from this underworld
where tortured souls cry out in anguish
behind bars of glass
so easy to break
yet impossible
blue eyes
hidden behind the glass and steel
strain to feel what the inhabited already know
what could be more naive
but I need you to
Charred black... voiceless
yet screaming your name
I need you to

KRISTIN AUGHENBAUGH

Release

Forever
Forever was my reminder of how long it took to get here
As I stared into my blue sky distorted by the light you held between your fingers
the fire you hid behind your eyes
As I take this breath it holds a hundred memories
What's only more is a thousand possibilities
but the darkness looms too near
As I put my trust in you I step back for the flames you held so dear
Silence answers my pleas and I exhale
Logic answers your screams and you run
What's worse is the doubt I held between my fingers
but I watched it as it fled on a night cradled in loud silence
the night the rainstorm took us away
brought us to sea, swept away to a wasteland of barren thoughts
left us with nothing but sordid memories
screaming at the back of our heads, fragile as ice
It took only a moment to lose it all

KRISTIN AUGHENBAUGH

Silver

Such a tragic beauty as your hair flew in the wind
I watched it as it fell
Silver tendrils locked together for one last time
I can never explain what I really saw
I'm not even sure if we met
How can we be properly introduced... if you don't exist?
Yet flashes of silver gleam like a sword on this cold winter's morning
Pale skin embodies a simple truth
But lines are blurred as I step out into this white
And paleness masks my own
Whatever truths, if any, existed on this empty winter's morning
fell wordlessly... with a flash of silver

Kristin Aughenbaugh

Shreya Baid

A Note from the Author

My name is Shreya Baid. I am 12 years old and I am in eighth grade. I was born in India, live in Miami, Florida and I attend Sts. Peter and Paul Catholic School. I first got interested in poetry at the age of 10. One day my teacher spoke to the class about different types of poetry like limericks, haikus, free verse, rhyming poetry, etc. This got my attention and gave me the desire to write my own. Slowly my skills evolved and as they did, so did my interest. I get inspiration from my teachers, my friends and from nature. I am proud to report that I am always on the "First Honor Roll" at school and have received the "President's Award for Academic Excellence" every year. My other hobbies are: piano, singing, art, web designing, volleyball, and swimming. My parents encourage me to reach for my goals in life, and never to give up even if times get rough.

Beautiful

The moon had vanished,
And the sun is rising up from the horizon.
The sparkling white snow that was here
Is now melting away
It's a whole new day.

The water flows freely,
Connecting with the sun
I want to engulf myself around the clouds.
I want to feel the wind brush my face.
It's a whole new day.

The sun is blazing like an oven.
I stare at its tranquility.
The light of the sun is bouncing off the water.
Beautiful flowers are beginning to bloom.
It's a whole new day.

Shreya Baid

My Mom

I admire,
I admire,
Whom do I choose to admire?
I admire my mom.
Why, you ask?
Well, it's a really simple task.
She is fun, kind, and caring.
She is also very bearing.
She is my precious mother,
And she can't be replaced by any other.
She is strict,
Like a brick.
But I don't care,
The sweet, rich smell in her hair
I like how she is.
Like a flower or a kiss.
You can come and meet her later.
But make sure you know,
That she's a really good baker!

SHREYA BAID

Sally Sue

Sally Sue, Sally Sue,
There was nothing that she could do.

She tried to play,
But she wasn't in the mood.
She tried to jump,
But she acted very crude.

She tried to pay attention,
She tried to speak.
But the sink,
Started to leak

So there she sat,
Bored and tired.
She couldn't think,
Of anything that she desired

She yelled and screamed.
She kicked and pounced.
She found a ball,
But it refused to bounce.

Sally Sue, Sally Sue,
There was nothing that she could do.

Shreya Baid

Rachel Bernhardt-Licea

Rachel Bernhardt-Licea was born on January 11, 1995 in Mercy Hospital located in Miami, Florida. Rachel likes to do cheerleading, cross-country, basketball, track and softball. She hopes to be a research doctor or a pediatrician.

We Give It All We Got

I am a cheerleader – watch me fly
I dance to the music and reach for the sky
You might not like it,
But my friends do and so do I
We give it all we got
As we tumble and fly

Rachel Bernhardt-Licea

Michael Cano

Michael Andrew Cano was born on July 29, 1992 in Miami, Florida, only 3 1/2 weeks before Hurricane Andrew. His mother is Soledad Schneegans Cano born in Nicaragua and his father is Jorge C. Cano born in Cuba. He is almost 5 years older than his sister Christina Nicole Cano. Michael has been a student at Sts. Peter & Paul Catholic School since Kindergarten in 1997.

Michael is a good student, is talented in art, and enjoys playing sports. His favorite sports are basketball, tennis, and snow skiing; but he has also enjoyed baseball, soccer, karate, fishing, cross country and track and field. More than anything, Michael Cano enjoys nature, going to the beach, movies, games, vacations, and spending time with family.

Dwyane Wade

My favorite player is Dwyane Wade
He plays for Miami Dade
He's my favorite player on the Heat
His skills make others suffer defeat
I want to grow up to be just like him
And learn to jump up to the rim
I learned a lot of his good moves
Which in after school I do use
This player has shown me a whole lot
Like to fight for what you want with all you got

MICHAEL CANO

Leaky Harry

There is a legendary story about a boy named Leaky Harry
It's usually quite funny but sometimes quite scary
This boy had a disturbing but unique drinking problem
Whenever he drank something it leaked from the bottom
He went to the bathroom about twenty times a day
Some said he wasn't human but the government wouldn't say
Poor Leaky Harry lived like this all his life
Drinking all day and leaking all night
I'm sorry to say good bye for right now
But wait till my next poem about Betty the Cow.

MICHAEL CANO

The Sea

I feel happy and free
When I go on a boat to sea,
The water is still and calm
As I sit there and talk to my mom.
I enjoy seeing the sunset
The water and the sun just met.
I wait till dusk to dawn
To see the land is gone,
God is the only key
To making such a beautiful sea

MICHAEL CANO

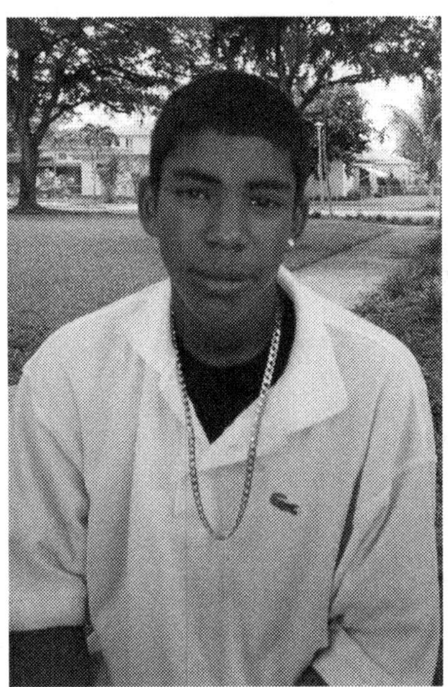

Mario Caraballo

Mario Caraballo was born in Miami Beach, Florida on May 1, 1992. He's the youngest of three children from parents Lilian and Tony Caraballo. Tony is the oldest and Melissa is the middle child. Mario is a very kind and respectful young man and very well liked by his family and friends.

Mario has always excelled in sports. He plays basketball year round. He is also very active in cross country, track and field and baseball. Mario's dad and older brother are active participants and often coach Mario's team.

Mario's favorite color is blue. He expressed the reason for blue being his favorite is because it is the color of the sky. Mario loves to swim in the pool with his best friends and family members. Pizza is his favorite food because of all the cheese. His most memorable moment was when he earned the biggest trophy he owns. It was awarded for being "Most Valuable Player" (M.V.P.) in the boys' basketball team at The Boys and Girls Club.

My Girlfriend

My beautiful girlfriend, she's the best
She talks to me with respect
She's pretty, nice, kind and sweet
Faithful to me and she won't cheat
We go to the movies to see some flicks
She is the hottest girl from all the chicks
Going to parties and dances too
There are no prettier girls than you
My girlfriend, I would love a kiss
Then happiness – delight!
I like everything about all girls
But for you my heart pumps and whirls

Mario Caraballo

Jacquelyn Conde

Jacquelyn Conde also known as Jackie was born on December 3, 1991 in Miami, Florida. Jackie is the youngest of four children. Her oldest sister Jessica, then brother Jason and sister Janelle are all of her siblings. Jackie loves to run and participated in cross country, plus track and field during earlier school years. She hopes to continue running in middle school and high school.

Nature Lover

Iguanas, butterflies and frogs
Are part of nature and life
Just like boys eating like hogs
In front of a husband and wife

Inside my house
You will find turtles and fish
Not a mouse going up a blouse
I have as many animals as I wish

Squirrels, crabs, dogs and cats
Also live in my home with me
Some of my pets even sleep on mats
If you come and visit you will see

Jacquelyn Conde

Valerie Corella

Valerie Corella was born on March 4, 1994 in Miami, Florida. She has four brothers named Ralph, Daniel, Michael and Dustin. Valerie also has two birds, one cat and a fish. Everyone that knows Valerie is pleased with her good manners, sweet nature and desire to please.

Valerie attends Shenandoah Middle School. She is participating in the Museum Magnet. Valerie enjoys reading and writing poems. Language Arts is her favorite subject and hopes to be an English/Literature teacher in the near future.

Valerie's parents hope that she will have a good and rewarding education. Valerie Corella lives with her father and grandmother. Valerie's mother lives in the Daytona area. Valerie likes to talk to some of her friends that live in Daytona once in a while. She says that she likes living in Miami a lot more than in Daytona because she has family and friends here. Valerie stated, "I like Daytona, but not as much as Miami."

Autobiography Poem

Valerie is my first name
Nice, humorous, smart and helpful I certainly am
Sister of Michael, Dustin, Ralph and Danny
They love me and I love them

Lover of music, swimming and reading
Feeling happy everyday, silly – or sad
Need shoes, clothes and a bank account
I keep reminding my mom and dad

I give gifts, money and supplies to the needy
And fear strangers, alligators and snakes
Would like to go to New York and have a party
With plenty of food, refreshments and cakes

I will own a house after graduating from college
As sure as Corella is my last name
I love Miami, family, friends and teachers
I say it proudly and not with shame

VALERIE CORELLA

Katryna Cruz

A Note from the Author

Hi my name is Katryna Cruz. I am 13 years old and I am in 8th grade. I love track and field and I am a cheerleader at the Comets All Stars. I also love to write when I am happy or even when I am feeling down. I have one sister named Tiffany and she is my everything. I love to laugh and also love being with my friends.

Why Have You Gone My Dearest Dawn?

I saw u standing there
And I would stare
We would laugh and play,
Until it came that day
Something happened and I had much fear
Right then I felt a tear
I knew she was gone when they told me...
"Your dearest dawn is gone."
Yet 'til this day my heart stays strong and it's all
Because I love your dawn – That terrible accident, my terrible fear...........
The fear you were no longer near

Katryna Cruz

Mila Dago

Hey! My name is Mila Anjelika Dago. I was born in Miami, Florida on March 14, 1991. I am 14 years old and attend La Salle High School. I am very athletic and like to do all kinds of sports. I am currently focusing on track & field and basketball. On my spare time I like to go out with my friends, read, write, talk on the phone, and use the computer. I am one of five children in my family. I am the middle child. My parents work very hard to get where they are today. In the future I wish to go to college at F.I.U or U.M. After college I would want to have a good paying career, get married and have kids.

Moon

Moon, people sometimes compare you
To a big ball of cheese,
To all those who like cheese,
You bring lots of glee.

I wish there was an elevator
Only accessed to me
That way when I'm upset
I can go up there to you
And clear my head
Then go to bed

Have you ever noticed,
How many friends you have?
Only 10 have names
The other are just burning flames
I bet you never get lonely

I want to thank you
For being my ever burning light
Always there for me at night
Always there shining bright

MILA DAGO

——> *Direction* <——

Sometimes I wish I can run away
I just want to keep running
Without choosing a way to go
Or a place to go
I just want to keep running
Without knowing which direction I'm going
Which way to turn
And whether to stop
Or keep on running
I just want to live without rules for once
Without having to listen to people nagging me on and on
Just for once to actually be able to take a breath and relax

MILA DAGO

Rene Dago

Rene Dago III was born on January 18, 1994 in Miami, Florida. He is the son of Rene Dago Jr. and Elvira Aedo Dago. Rene is the fourth of five children conceived from the same two parents. His siblings are Tahlia, Ursula, Mila and Giancarlo Dago.

Rene plays baseball, basketball, football and is also very active in cross country, track and field. He plays baseball year-round. Blue is his favorite color because it is the color of the sea. His most memorable moment was when he received his first sports' trophy ever.

Rene is an honor roll student. He is an avid reader. He also earned "Student of the Month" when he was in third grade. Rene will start Middle School in 2005. He plans to continue being active in sports, reading and writing.

My Gifts from God

My intelligence is useful for many things. As I am blessed with life which is a gift from God, so is my intelligence. I use my intelligence to think for tests, homework and schoolwork. If I hadn't been blessed with my intelligence; I would get nothing but "F's."

Another gift from God is my athletic ability. Athletic ability is great and comes in handy to perform in the sports that I enjoy. I am always in the game. When I grow up, I might even end up famous and rich! It doesn't matter if I am tall, young, slim or fat. I'm still an athlete, and that's that! I excel in all aspects of the game. It does not matter if I'm team captain or not, no matter what, only the coach makes the calls.

Rene Dago III

Picking Up My Room

Picking up my room
Makes me more tired than P.E.!
It is not fun to do
My dad often tells me
To clean up before going to a game
Don't want to do it
So he tells me, "What a shame!"
Meanwhile I just frown and sit
While my teammates get a bat to hit
My dad finally gives in
And helps me

Rene Dago III

Andrew Davis

Andrew Joel Davis was born July 25th, 1990. He attended Silver Bluff Elementary School from kindergarten through second grade and participated in the Academic Excellence Program. He then transferred to Coral Gables Elementary School for third through fifth grade in order to take advantage of the full time Gifted Program.

For the middle school grades he attended Riviera Middle School where he excelled in mathematics advancing two years ahead. Andrew Davis presently attends Southwest Senior High School and is in the tenth grade. He is currently a member of the school's cross-country team. Andrew has won awards in piano and the FCAT math. Andrew received the maximum score in the FCAT math last year in the ninth grade.

The Game

My first game ever
I pulled the lever
To get into the gate
Without any fate
I grabbed my fries
We know all must rise,
For the Star-Spangled Banner
The jets flew by in an orderly manner
We were winning the game
The players weren't playing for fame
It was a big crowd,
It got very loud
The game was fun to watch
The stadium turned up a notch
As time ran out,
We were all cheering about
Three, two, one
The game is done!

Andrew Joel Davis

Annette Elguezabal

Annette Victoria Elguezabal was born on March 4th, 1996 in Miami, Florida. She is currently in the fourth grade. Annette lives with her two parents Eddy and Virginia Elguezabal and has a five year old brother named Eddy. She takes pleasure in music and dancing. She also enjoys playing the violin and is part of a music bucket group at school. In the summer months Annette benefits from camping and swimming.

Life Is a Mystery

Life is a mystery
When you are happy or sad
Throughout your whole life
You should be glad

Life is a mystery
Surprised by a pie
When the kitchen door opens
And it's my dad with a tie

Life is a mystery
Whether you are skinny or fat
When my brother hits a homerun
With a ball and a bat

Life is a mystery
When my mother hugs me
I know that I'm loved
And I jump with glee

Annette Elguezabal

Christina Fernandez

Christina Fernandez is currently nine years old. She has a younger sister and Gus is her older brother who lives in Okinawa, Japan. Christina loves to be creative; whether it is dancing ballet, singing a tune or drawing her fantasies. She loves to explore, spend time with her dog "Cocco" and always seeks to be with nature.

Alaska

Flowers are blooming,
Sky is clean
Life over there is beautiful –
Whales, dolphins swimming in the sea
Mountains with snow on the ground
People look somewhat different
But they are always welcoming

CHRISTINA FERNANDEZ

Cocco

Cocco is fluffy, cottony white
Cocco is a handsome male
Cocco is adorable and cute
Cocco is a Maltese puppy
Cocco is a loyal friend
Cocco is my puppy

CHRISTINA FERNANDEZ

Eli Fernandez

Hi, my name is Eli Fernandez. I am 13 and a 7th grader at Sts. Peter and Paul Catholic School. I enjoy many sports such as basketball and cheerleading. I especially love cheerleading. I cheer for my school and for an All-Star team. On my school team I am the captain and I have also become an All-American Cheerleader for four years in a row. I hope to attend La Salle or Mast Academy. When I am older I wish to become a lawyer or a fashion designer. If I become a fashion designer then my designs will probably be pink. Pink is my favorite color. :)

The Week of a Lazy Person

Call me lazy but according to me
The school week is getting as dull as can be
Monday's a challenge
Tuesday's a bore
Wednesday's a handful
And Thursday's just more
Friday's the best because there's nothing ahead
Except Saturday and Sunday when I sleep in my bed

Eli Fernandez

Juan Figueroa

Juan Figueroa was born on July 5, 1995 in Miami, Florida. He likes to play football. He hopes to be a professional football player in the future. His favorite color is blue and his favorite food is pizza.

Moms

Moms are special
Everyone knows
Feelings are not artificial
They are as gentle as a rose

My mom is caring
She is also loving and kind
Even when I don't behave and I'm daring
No wonder they say love is blind

Juan Figueroa

Brittany Fowler

A Note from the Author

I am 15 years old and currently a sophomore at St. Petersburg High School in the International Baccalaureate Program. I do everything a typical teenager likes to do and I am always with my friends or family. My weekends are filled with shopping, movies, and beaches. I enjoy being active in school activities and I'm always staying busy.

I have been writing poetry and short stories for about four years now, but I have always had a passion for writing. I get my inspiration to write from many things in life, from friends, family and enemies, life struggles, dreams, God and love. Writing is a wonderful way for me to express myself and I hope to always continue my poetic and writing development.

Fall from Grace

I wonder if it hurt her
Falling from the heavens
Yet illuminating this dark,
Dreary world with only a smile
Shining her light upon us all,
Casting away the whimsical shadows
And blessing us with her warmth;
One solitary angel, alone, and yet alive
Instilling fear with her beauty
And encasing hope within her heart
Spreading joy with her presence,
Telling truths with nothing but a gaze
But becoming belittled by her surrounding,
Yet standing tall among giants and kings;
Her eyes how do they still shimmer?
Despite her broken halo and drooping wings,
Replaced by sinners' crown of thorns
And a heavy burden upon her fragile back
And she still brushes away her tears
And lets them spiral to the earth
Creating puddles of hope for those that trudge on;
Now I know why she cries
She misses heaven and its magical grace
Left here, no path to follow along
Wandering among all that is unholy
Streaming those tears that sprinkle a bit of her
Grace and color into this dull world,
Yet the angel still maintains her smile...
And you would never know she hated it here,
That she wants to ascend back into the graces
But she'll never give up hope,
And she'll never fly away,
She'll continue her melancholy march
Here on earth, to save us with her grace

Brittany Fowler

In a Matter of Moments

?All in a matter of moments
?All in a matter of moments

Deep in an unconscious sleep
A man lies alone in bed
Playing with the thoughts he keeps
All locked up in his head

Evils rang of his words and lies,
And the shifty company he kept,
Unaware his life would pass him by
So all the while he slept

?All in a matter of moments
?All in a matter of moments

Ignorant to the realities
Of how he was being judged,
Caught up with the superficialities
Always forgetting his creator above

Lived paralyzed to all that was holy
He was caught, nothing he could do
He finally realized all that could be,
And fought to get up and start anew

? All in a matter of moments
?All in a matter of moments

The truth came crashing down upon him
It was too late, his time was up
The lord was a forgiving god, and
He was already given time to grow up

Etched with a mood so somber,
Still and full of utter dread;
Nothing can awake this slumber
?For the man was already dead

?All in a matter of moments
?All in a matter of moments

Should have went to church more,
Didn't the years hold enough time?
Should have praised the lord,
Then he'd be in heavens sublime

If only he had more time with less haste
I would have a different story to tell,
But a man's life here has gone to waste,
Cast down to the bowels of hell

?All in a matter of moments
?All in a matter of moments

His *all* was lost in moments,
Moments he chose to throw away;
He traveled far from the divine end
When he chose to go the other way

So live your life to the fullest
But don't forget the light above,
It will pass in a matter of moments,
And before you know it you'll be judged

?All in a matter of moments
?All in a matter of moments

BRITTANY FOWLER

Paul George

Paul George is the son of Dr. Paul George and Laura George. He is the oldest of three siblings. Matthew is the middle brother and Mary Rose is the younger sister. Paul was 13 years old when he wrote these poems.

Paul George goes to a Catholic School in Miami, Florida. He is an honor roll student and earned the prestigious award in the National Junior Honor Society. Paul has been playing tennis for almost nine years and is in the league of the United States Tennis Association. He plays football. He has been running in cross-country and track and field for three years. Paul is a very well-rounded child. He is very responsible, reliable, excels in academic achievement, is very sociable with his peers and is a true athlete.

The Game You Choose

Tennis is a great sport
You have to play on a court
I've been playing since I was six
And I might know a few tricks.
When the ball hits my racket,
It's like fifty pounds of air.
Maybe you can say that's fair.
It's not whether you win or lose;
It's having fun with the game you choose!

PAUL GEORGE

Pets

There's great responsibility when it comes to handling a pet,
Like when it gets sick, you'll have to take it to the vet.
So if you have a dog,
You'll have to take it outside for a pee. But it doesn't matter
That wouldn't bother me
Your pet is acting like a beast?
Do not bother giving it its feast
Always watch out for your pet
And if you do that, you'll be all set.

Paul George

Acelia Gonzalez

Facts about the Author

Date of birth:	02/12/91
Place of birth:	Miami, FL
Daughter of:	Xiomara Duarte
Brothers:	Alain and Abel Martell
Sisters:	Aimara Gonzalez and Andria Martell
Hobbies:	Shopping, meeting new friends, and my cell
Likes:	Cheerleading, and dancing flamenco
Favorite movie:	The Notebook
Favorite colors:	Red, silver and pink

Please Don't Let Me

Please don't let me fall in love with him again in his talk of sweet.
Where his eye twinkle like a star into mines.
Don't let me fall for his unforgettable lips that once touched mines but have been shut forever without a kiss goodbye.
He will touch my face and call my name and I will burn with desire.
Don't let me forget what he did to me and the knowing of another.
I want to navigate his mind all the time and never let him forget he was once mine.
Like in the early morning, fog hanging like old coats between the trees let me wander off into my dreams, and forget he sees in another girl's eye. Let me not fall for someone whose love is not for me.

ACELIA GONZALEZ

Tears Fading

Memories, friendship seems to all fade away, why does it have to end this way? Tears drip down my face because instantly we seem to fade away,
We use to be tighter night and day
At night flashes of memories begin to echo in my head and remembering
You saying I love you,
Please say you do
But don't lie
Hurting me will just make me cry

Acelia Gonzalez

Brian Gonzalez

Brian Joseph Gonzalez was born on February 13th, 1994, four weeks before has was expected. Brian weighed only six pounds two ounces, but was nineteen inches long. His mother, Indira Gomez-Gonzalez was born in Cuba and his father Jose L. Gonzalez was born in New Orleans. Brian is the eldest of two; therefore, he has a young brother Justin Michael, who is four years old.

Brian is currently attending South Miami Middle School. Brian is a participant of the "Chorus Magnet Program." Obviously, Brian loves to sing and perform. Brian is a good student, who was an honor roll student throughout his elementary school years. He hopes to continue his academic achievement and in the future become a very successful, wealthy attorney or engineer. Brian enjoys playing chess and sports like tennis, soccer, and basketball. Brian also enjoys going to the beach, movies, games, vacations and spending time with his family.

Autumn

October is finally here!
Come and celebrate the holidays
Together we can go
Out trick or treating and
Be safe and stay away from strangers
Everyone will have lots of fun!
Running around in a costume on Halloween

Brian Gonzalez

Dodger

I have a huge dog
Dodger is his name
He eats like an enormous hog
Then we play a game
Together we jump and run
I use my two and he uses four
This is so much fun
It makes me feel rich, not poor
Dodger is my special friend
I know he thinks the same
If he gets hurt, I help it mend
My dog is not wild, he is tame
I love my puppy
Much better than my guppy!

BRIAN GONZALEZ

Peace

Let there be peace on Earth
So that we can live on a better turf
The more peace the less trouble
So let the peace double.
Wars need to end
So we finally can mend
All our troubles

Brian Gonzalez

Elisa Gonzalez

Elisa Gonzalez was born on October 15, 1991 in Miami, Florida. Elisa is a very spirited teenager that loves to chat online, talk on the phone, and hang out with friends. Most of all she enjoys drawing and painting. Elisa attends Design and Architecture Senior High (D.A.S.H) where she plans to go in the fashion industry.

Don't Let Fear Interfere

It started out so wrong
On a hot summer day
I was with my two friends
And "the boy" passed my way
Not just any boy…
Suddenly all these feelings
From my past all replayed
Not much to look at
Others would say
If only they looked at it my way
My past he held in his eyes
He approached me
His eyes staring into mine
Destiny played once again
As we realized we needed each other
Things went great
He was all I could think about
There was no doubt
Silence did not exist in our own little world
Communication was surely there
When I was with him,
My shyness was erased
In a room full of people
It felt like if we were alone
The feeling was mutual …
Suddenly thoughts from our past relationship
Rushed through my spirit
And filled me with negativity and fear
Should have trusted the moment
Not what happened a year ago
An act of selfishness
Due to inner fears –
Not wanting to endure pain once again
Out of impulse,
I set him on the side,
Only thinking of myself

A decision that I now regret,
My dear loved one I was forced to forget
A wrong choice ended it wrong...
In the future I will know better
Not to let my fears rule
And I will remember
My own set of words,
"Don't let fear interfere."

Elisa Gonzalez

Roxana Iviricu

Roxana Iviricu was born on April 17, 1996. She likes to draw a lot. She also loves to eat. Her favorite foods are meat, rice and apples. Her favorite subject is mathematics.

I like...

I like to play
I always say
Hopscotch and jump rope
With my favorite friends Jessica and Hope

I like to eat
Rice and meat
With my brother and father
Mother and grandmother

I like to read
And water the seed
With my nice neighbor
We do hard labor

Roxana Iviricu

Dakota R. Lipton

A Note from the Author

My name is Dakota R. Lipton. I go to G.W. Carver Middle School. I am now in the 7th grade. I am from Miami, Florida, born on March 10, 1993. I have two sisters and no brothers. My favorite subject in school is mathematics. I like to play basketball, volleyball, tennis, softball and I also like to dance. My goals in life are to get better in my dancing so I can become professional or to get better in acting so I can become an actress.

Star Gazing

Lying in the hammock gazing at the stars,
I wonder if the one by the moon is Mars;
And why some stars shine so bright,
While others are tiny specks in the night
Sitting back in my chair as I stare fly by;
People say to wish on the first one,
But I think you should wish on everyone.

Dakota R. Lipton

Swinging

I just love swinging!
When I swing I feel like I am flying in the air.
When I feel like I'm flying in the air I get a feeling that I am free.
When I feel like I am free I feel like I can do anything I want.
When I feel like I can do anything I want I feel like I am special and trusted.

Dakota R. Lipton

The Cozy Bed

Everyday when I raise my sleepy head,
I have to say good-bye to my cozy bed.

My bed is always there when I'm ready to fall,
Into the pillows and blankets I crawl.

Can't wait to come back to see you again,
But there's a lot to do between now and then.

Dakota R. Lipton

Sasha Martinez

Sasha Martinez was born on February 14, 1991 in Miami, Florida. She is the daughter of Maria del Carmen Gonzalez and Luis Martinez. Christian Martinez is older brother. Sasha is a very popular teenager that loves to play softball and volleyball. She also enjoys cheerleading. Sasha is a high school student attending La Salle.

All Because of You

Because of you I realized
There is no happily ever after
Did you think that all the lies
Would fly right by me
Then once found out
You'd beg for forgiveness
Or would continue lying
Through your teeth you would plea
"For what, more lack of trust!"
That would give me further
Bitter taste of disgust
What a cheater, what a dog
Tears that meant something
My heart that would go – zing
Breaking my kindness with a sling
Go on with your merry, shallow ways
For me, I shall have joyous days
Apart from you with someone else
Who will cherish me and offer
What I do deserve – trust, truth, love
I realized and learned
All because of you

SASHA MARTINEZ

No Boyfriend, No Problem

Boys can be nice, boys can be funny
But why get tied down
When they can break your heart
And make your nose runny
Instead have a blast with no worries
Go out on the town
Make sure to be smart
Boyfriends, who needs them
When you are young and alive
One wrong choice could ruin your life
No boyfriend, no problem!

Sasha Martinez

Alberto Monnar

A Note from the Author

The most incredible day of my life was the day I was born. I came to life on November 8, 1990 in Wayne County, Michigan. I describe myself as a funny, annoying and sometimes shy guy. I am handsome and girls like me. I like one girl at a time and it's usually the same one for a long period of time meaning years.

My favorite movie is "The Notebook" even though I'm a guy and not a lot of guys like romantic movies. My favorite kind of music is rap with rappers such as Ludacris and Mike Jones. The computer is another tool I love. Visiting the Florida Marlins or Miami Heat Web sites are way cool. You can see the statistics on how each player compares to the next. I'm frequently chatting online with my friends, playing video games or building future cities. My five most important things to me are: God, family, basketball, friends and girlfriend.

I live for sports! In my spare time you will find me practicing or playing basketball year-round. If dreams came true, I would want to be a famous basketball player and make a lot of money. My back-up plan is to get a degree in teaching and become a physical education coach. My mother always says I would make a wonderful engineer, C.P.A., city planner or anything related to math because that is my strongest subject, next to P.E. But she says that I can be anything I wish to be. The important thing is to enjoy what you are doing so that your occupation is not just a job.

My sister Anna and brother Alex are both younger. I am the oldest sibling living in our home. I also have an older sister Alina who is a flight attendant. She is my half sister from my dad's side. I love, care and like my mom and family. Since I grow so quickly, I give my clothes away to others less fortunate.

The Girl Who Only Loved Herself

This story begins with a young girl who was ten years old. She would always make fun of people because of the way they looked. She thought she was the most beautiful girl in the world. She was born in the big city, New York. Her name was Maggie. Maggie never shared or helped anybody. But one day it all changed. Read some more and find out what or whom changed her life.

"Maggie wake up!" her mom said from the kitchen. It's time for school. Maggie was really mad because she had no friends and her dad was out of town. When Maggie went to eat breakfast her mom asked her if she had slept well. Maggie never answered her.

A few minutes later Maggie heard the bus. Her mom always gave her a ham and cheese sandwich. "Hurry the bus is leaving Maggie go!" said her mom. When she got on the bus there were two kids named Jake and Philip, they looked at her with a strange face. They were mad at her because she would always make fun of them. Maggie would always tell them that their hair was messy, or they were too fat, or their glasses were too big.

When they got to school she looked angry and aggravated. On the first day of school she told the teacher that she wanted to sit away from all the nerds, and that she was too beautiful to sit with them. Everyday she was so mean to everyone. She was even nasty to Mrs. Jenny. Mrs. Jenny is Maggie's teacher. Maggie is in fifth grade. The next class that Maggie went to was her favorite class which was math. She was the smartest in her class so she felt too smart next to the other kids. Math class was the only class that Maggie was actually good at. It would always make her feel good.

Two hours later it was P.E. time. She was also good at P.E. She was the fastest one in her class. But every time they would have to run she would make fun of the other kids. Her coach was named Mr. Williams but everyone called him Coach Williams. He was not too happy about this.

Lunch was next. She always sat by herself because she didn't let anybody sit next to her. She called it the popular table. She was the only popular one because she was the only one who sat there. When it was time to leave, Maggie's mom went up to Mrs. Jenny and asked her if Maggie did well today but she said, "No." in a polite way.

After school when Maggie and her mom got home, Maggie's mom calls Maggie and tells her that they are going to meet her great-grandma. Maggie has never seen her great-grandma before. In the car Maggie wanted to find out if her great-grandma was beautiful or not. When they got there, Maggie couldn't believe her eyes. She saw the ugliest person ever. At least that is what Maggie thought at the moment. Her great-grandma was a little upset because she heard some nasty things about Maggie. She asked Maggie to sit and talk with her on the couch.

At first Maggie was a little nervous because she has never had an actual conversation with anyone. Maggie's great-grandmother was very wise and told Maggie many things that made a difference. Maggie said to her, "I am so sorry."

Then her great grandma replied to her in a soft voice, "It is okay child." Maggie and her great grandma had the longest conversation in their lives especially Maggie. The great-grandma didn't look so ugly to Maggie anymore. Maggie started seeing things differently from that moment on.

When her mom called her to leave, Maggie said bye to her great-grandma and gave her a big hug, Maggie's mom was so surprised when she saw Maggie and her great- grandma like that. In the car Maggie's mom asked Maggie a question and Maggie answered her question for the first time. Maggie's mom felt like the luckiest mom in the world. Something the great-grandma said to Maggie made a difference in her attitude. Maggie changed her attitude from very bad to very good.

A month later Maggie was getting along with everyone and she had nearly 15 friends including the nerds. The popular table no longer existed so Maggie and her friends moved to that table.

At night she heard knocking on the door when she went to open the door it was her dad which she had not seen for almost a year. Maggie really never talked to her dad either so when she went to give him a hug her dad got so happy he started crying. Maggie's dad said to her with tears coming out of his eyes, "I missed you cupcake!"

The next morning Maggie saw her parents crying. Maggie said to them, "What is wrong?"

They replied, "Your great-grandma passed away." From that day on, Maggie never forgot that one special day she had with her great-grandma.

Alberto Monnar

Special People

Special people are good and nice
While eating black beans and white rice
I love my mother and she loves me too
When I'm happy or feeling blue

My dad died and went to Heaven
Got sick when I was eleven
Special father in my heart
Taught me things because he was smart

Family members are special
From the time born to burial
I love my sisters and brother
My grandfather and grandmother

Aunts, uncles, lots of cousins too
Help us, guide us and see us through
Friends similar to family
Are special! Elementary!

Alberto Monnar

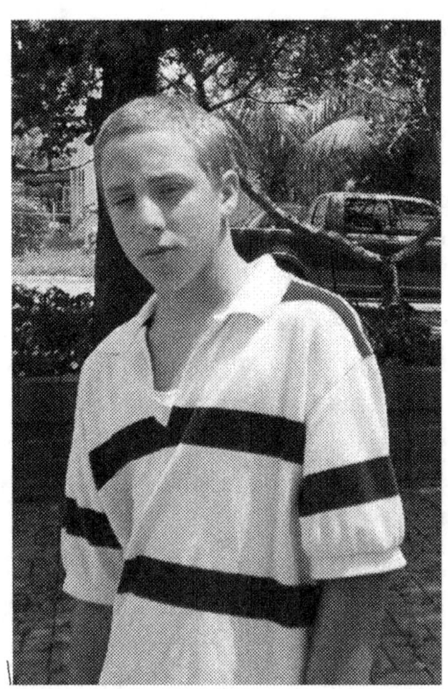

Alexander Monnar

Alexander Monnar was born in Miami, Florida on August 21, 1991. He's funny, athletic and entertaining. Alexander enjoys participating in team sports, especially basketball. He loves to watch the Miami Heat, Florida Marlins and Tiger Woods on television.

Alex is quite a ladies' man, loves to talk on the telephone and chat online with his friends. Alexander's sense of humor reminds his mother of Eddie Murphy. He can be quite amusing once you get to know him.

Alex can put together any furniture that comes unassembled and fix things around the home. He loves to go to the movies, parties and visit his best friend Mario's home. To know Alex is to love Alex.

Annoying Alex

Once upon a time there was a five year old boy named Alex. His family always used to tell him, "Alex, stop being so annoying!" From the moment Alex would wake up he would love to annoy his mother. He would love to annoy his sister. He would love to annoy his brother. Alex seemed to get pleasure from annoying anyone and everyone.

Alex went in his room and started to throw clothes on the floor. Then he started to jump on his brother's bed. Every time after doing all of the annoying things, Alex would ask his mom, "Do you love me?" His mother would always answer, "Yes I do Alex, but I don't like what you are doing!"

His mother was calling him and he didn't want to come. He was throwing his toys and his games. His mother called him five more times. Alex's mother was about to suffer from a heart attack. Finally, he went to eat breakfast.

Alex sat down on his chair by the table. He started throwing cereal at his brother and sister. Alex's sister was telling him to stop. Alex said, "No!" Then Alex's sister told on him and his mom informed Alex that he could not play with the computer.

Alex went to school and sat down in the classroom. He started throwing pencils at the teacher.

The teacher said, "Stop Alex!"

Then Alex said, "Okay."

The bell rang and Alex went to physical education, art and lunch. During all the other subjects he sat quietly, did his work and was just fine. When he went back to homeroom he started throwing pencils again to the teacher.

The teacher said, "Go to the principal's office."

Alex went straight down to the principal's office and sat down. There was nobody there so he waited. He was still waiting. It had been 30 minutes after the teacher told him to go to the office and still nobody came. Alex thought about all the bad stuff he had done. After thinking for quite a while he finally realized that he loved pushing people's buttons. It must be that he had control of how some people would react and not some others. He really got joy from those who would react to his annoying ways.

After giving it more thought, Alex realized that he was acting like a brat. He figured out that by being annoying he would only get punishment and would get grounded. Then he decided, I am going to hug my brother for what I did, my sister, my mom, and my teacher. He was really sorry for being so annoying and realized that it was best to get people's attention through kindness and good actions.

So when it was time to leave Alex said to his teacher, "I am sorry that I threw the pencils." Then, Alex gave her a hug and the teacher forgave him. Alex went home and said, "Sorry" to his brother and gave him a hug. Alex went to his sister and said, "Sorry" and gave her a hug. Alex went to his mom and said, "Sorry" and gave her a hug. The family forgave Alex.

It was amazing that even though Alex did all of the annoying things, everyone accepted his apology and forgave him. He seemed to be sincere about really thinking and making an effort to control himself from then on. He went home and entered his bedroom. Alex looked at the crucifix in his room and said, "I am sorry to Jesus Christ the Son of God." He then picked up the mess in his room, cleaned up and thought and thought. After thinking for quite a while, he thought that it was time to grow up and to be kinder to people.

ALEXANDER MONNAR

My Best Friend

My best friend Mario, he's so cool
He's my buddy at home and school
We dribble up and down the court
Basketball is the hottest sport
Mario's family is good to me
In land, air and the deep blue sea
His mom and dad are way awesome
Feed us well so we can blossom
His sister Melissa looks so hot
She's kind and sweet and hugs a lot
Melissa's smile will make you melt
Just like ice-cream dripping on your belt
The big brother's name is Tony
Eats pizza with pepperoni
Athletic and tall and can dunk
Pretty girls say he's quite a hunk
My family loves Mario too
With us, he's part of the loved crew
We go to restaurants to eat
The best part is dessert; it's so sweet
Best friends are special in many ways
Sharing the beach with the sun's rays
Enjoying life is worth our time
Otherwise it's not worth a dime
We giggle, laugh and act like fools
However, we do follow rules
Having a best friend is so good
Let me know if you understood

Alexander Monnar

Anna Monnar

Anna Lee Monnar is the daughter of Ana and Octavio Monnar. Along with her brothers Alberto and Alexander, she is also blessed with an older sister, Alina, from Mr. Monnar's first marriage. Anna was born in Harris, New York on June 24, 1991. Anna is very much loved by her family and friends.

Anna took many years of dance lessons. From age 4 to age 11, she danced ballet, lyrical, tap and jazz. She reads the second reading during mass every month. She loves and participates in track and field, cross country, basketball, softball volleyball, and enjoys being in team sports at school.

Anna Lee Monnar started writing poetry and short stories since an early age. Anna's mother and Mrs. Alvarez, the literature teacher inspired her to compose different types of poems. Both ladies played a key role in encouraging Anna to compile poems in her journal. Anna Lee Monnar illustrated her first book titled, *La ley del embudo The Law of the Funnel: A Bilingual Story.* A mother and daughter collaboration, this book explores the themes of selfishness and giving in a global setting. Anna will be starting high school August of 2005. To read more about Anna Lee Monnar please visit www.readersareleadersusa.net/illustrator.html whenever time permits.

Bright Moon

Star light star bright the moon – a firefly
At night it brings you natural light
When all is not bright have no fear the moon
Is there to wipe your tears throughout your precious years – The moon is a white orchid growing out of the deep blue sea
It is the romantic part of a couple
Up on a hill by a tree
It is the lamp at night that glows and shines
It is a wonderful view when you are above the water under a sky of stars and a delightful moon full of light to brighten your night Another signal for when the moon is out is When the kids shout because they – Hear the dogs howl – So when you are having a bad day – Have no worries just wait a while and the moon will give you a great big smile
Now I know why the cow jumped over the moon – It was to catch the view from a better sight –
The light of the moon can make it all right

Anna Lee Monnar
Thanks Mrs. Alvarez for guiding and motivating us to write.

Mother and Daughter

Mother and Daughter
Don't brothers get jealous?

Shopping together into girls' great palace
Mothers and daughters always laughing together
Telling little girls stories and jokes to the mother
Mother and daughter there's nothing much to it
Just live with each other and trust one another

And
Hey mother how come you never spend as much time with me?
Oh I knew my brother was jealous of me!

Anna Lee Monnar

Rapid Waterfall

To my mom – thanks for inspiring me to write

Rapid waterfall
Flowing to the shallow pond
Pearls beneath each rock
Children splashing all day long
watch the fish swim up and down
Splish splash, hear the kids laugh
tiring their little selves out
now the fish can rest in peace
while the children fall asleep
Feel the breeze against your cheeks
while you take a walk beside the waterfall

Anna Lee Monnar

Tiffany Marie Oharriz

Tiffany Oharriz was born on July 3, 1989 in Hialeah Hospital to Mirta and William Oharriz. Since the age of five, Tiffany has been writing poetry, singing, acting and dancing. Tiffany has accomplished earning poet of the year, a creative poetry award. She was featured in six books and the sound of poetry CD in more than three separate occasions.

Tiffany loves sports including: softball, basketball, and volleyball. But her greatest passion next to musical theater and astronomy is poetry. Tiffany Marie Oharriz also acted in many plays and competitions and has been singing for numerous years. She plans to major in musical theater and minor in astronomy thanks to Mrs. Nuñez and Mr. H.

My So-Called Life

Why must I live among a family...
That rays her glory upon me.
I live in her shadows...
Everyday
I cry and weep
and sit and pray.
She's been gone since I was four.
She died... she died of cancer and no more.
They led me to believe,
I wasn't meant to be.
It's my fault they say
she died because of me.
So I sit and pray
And hope and say
That some day
They'll love me for me,
And that I was meant to be.

TIFFANY MARIE OHARRIZ
"My sister is my inspiration and mother's memory; it is what keeps me going."

Kahyra Paulete

About the Author

Kahyra Paulete was born in Montevideo, Uruguay on October 29, 1993. She loves to play tennis, play basketball, dance and loves to have fun with friends. Kahyra is currently a student in G.W Carver middle school in sixth grade.

Mother

I love my mother oh so much, the
way she cooks and bakes.
To feel her loving hands that touch
my face, my heart she takes away.
Sometimes I do things and she gets
mad it's not for long but even so.
I get upset and then I'm sad. She
kisses me and my love grows.

Kahyra Paulete

Why?

Why was I born
Asked a girl outdoors
why do animals exists
Asked a boy in his seat
Why am I here today
Asked Andres everyday
Why are you here asking
so many questions
When you could be in the park
having a fun time!

KAHYRA PAULETE

Andres (Andy) Quinta

Andres (Andy) R. Quinta wrote the following poems at age 13. He was born on October 2, 1991. It was 12:32 P.M. at Mercy Hospital where he arrived. Andres R. Quinta is now 5'4" tall and weighs 100 pounds. His favorite color is red and his favorite sports are baseball, basketball, tennis, track and field and swimming. Andy enjoys going to dance parties and chatting on the internet with friends.

The Quinta Family loves pets. They have two dogs named Shirley and Beethoven, 12 cockatiels, two hermit crabs named "El Gringo" and "Sponge Bob." In addition to all of their pets there is Belinda, the mom, Andy, the dad and Adrian the little brother, plus big brother Andy.

Andres earned the prestigious Junior Honors Society award. His favorite vacation was a trip to North Carolina. Andy exclaimed, "My most memorable moment, "I hit a *Grand Slam* in a very important baseball tournament in Dreams Park at Cooperstown, N.Y."

Basketball

Now basketball is my favorite sport
I like the way they dribble up and down the court.
I keep it so fresh on the microphone;
No interruptions when the game's on.
I like slam dunks that take me to the hoop;
My favorite play is the ally-hoop. I like the pick and roll
I like the give and go and basketball bounce, bounce lets go.

Andres Quinta

Hilarious Poem

In the meadow, or in the hood,
Go and buy yourself some food.

At the mall or in your car,
Think of me, I can't be far.

Over at a friend's or asleep in your house,
A boy should never wear a woman's blouse.

Feeling sad or a little ashamed,
Go and buy a golden chain.

In a party or at the clubs,
Hit me up, I'll buy some subs.

Andres Quinta

My Life

I like to dance,
I like to chill,
Going to parties,
My face in a glance

Staying home and being bored,
Makes me feel, like I'm all torned
Baseball is my hobby, y'all better respect,
You can never challenge me;
I'll put you to the test.

Andres Quinta

Daniel Rams

Daniel Julius Rams was born in Miami, Florida. He was a fifth grade student when he wrote this poem. Daniel lives with his mother and sister, and enjoys fishing in his free time. Daniel's favorite sport is basketball and hopes one day to be an NBA player.

Animal Game

My opponent says
I play like a cat
But I can defeat him
Because he is a rat

Daniel Rams

Michael Jordan

Michael Jordan – a great man
Basketball player of the NBA
As a boy he played sports,
Baseball, football and a lot more
He won rookie of the year,
Before he retired from his career
Michael Jordan loved his dad
When he was murdered he became sad
Michael Jordan played baseball
For the memory of his dad
But then decided to return,
To the sport he would yearn
Basketball, Basketball,
Best of all!

Daniel Rams

Victoria Rams

Victoria Irene Rams was born in Miami, Florida. She was a third grade student when she wrote this poem. Victoria lives with her mother and brother. Her favorite subject is art. Victoria likes art best because she expresses her creativity with much success. Victoria hopes one day to be an artist.

That's That!

I love my mom,
I love my dad,
I love my whole family
Even my cat,
Even my brother
That bothers me a lot
He is still my brother
And that's that!

VICTORIA RAMS

Catherine Ries

A Note from the Author

I was born in New Port Beach, California on November 7, 1989. I moved to Wisconsin when I was 8 years old and attended St. Sebastian's Middle School. Then after graduating I went to Pius XI High School where I will be a sophomore next school year. And I plan on pursuing my studies in language, English, and art. I've wanted to become an archaeologist for as long as I can remember, so hopefully I'll get into that too.

Some hobbies of mine are playing guitar, which I've been playing for about 4 years now. I also enjoy painting, playing

Frisbee (a new passion of mine), and dancing. Just full on crazy out of control dancing. I live with my father, and sister, and 2 cats. We recently had 3 frogs but my dad decided to "liberate" them into the river nearby.

I love music, singing, dancing, poetry, art, reading, social hacking, galaxies, dread locks, thunderstorms, chocolate, people watching, facial hair, accents, hands, and water. I don't like people who never change, grow, or evolve (i.e. people who complain yet never do anything to change it.) Thieves and liars, social exhibitionists, people who think that bathroom humor is a really good idea. Flakes, people who don't relate to the idea of certain words really freaking someone out, like me. I'm not about to disclose my list here.

I love just hanging around by myself, or with friends, doing absolutely nothing. Most of my friends don't really throw parties, and if they did I probably wouldn't go because I much rather like going to festivals or shows to watch bands play so I can dance and just hang out, like Milwaukee's Summerfest. Where I can dance as much as I want and eat good food, dancing is the best thing in the world. Just recently I went to Summerfest with my cousins who I hadn't seen in 4 years, and my 25 year old cousin Brendan is really into Reggae music and we went to see King Solomon and Steel Pulse.

Man-o-man, it was so much fun, there were all these Rastafarians everywhere with dreadlocks and just dancing. And some guy who looked like a young Bob Marley taught me how to dance reggae-style. Just a few more moves to add to my repertoire. And I have way too many favorites movies which I have listed somewhere and its a couple pages long, so I won't even start to list them here. My time usually isn't spent watching TV, but when I do, I watch Family Guy, the Simpson's, X-Files, Seinfeld, and Arrested Development (too bad it was cancelled.)

Because Every Movie You're in Becomes My Favorite

Not idol, never say idol.
That is not a description highly loved.
But rather, use descriptions of your own
For mine are tainted with other thoughts
Dreams, Obsession, Fantasies
I'd like to think I'm better than the other millions out there. That if I came face to face with my obsession I would stay calm, cool, collected. Discuss art, theater and poetry over a cup of coffee. But I don't even drink coffee. My visions of the moonlit lobby of an abandoned hotel in Paris Of the ferns in the corner, the pale green sofas on the red wine rug – The phone booths in the west wall, screened in by glass doors – The counter, with coffee and cappuccino makers behind it. Brass bar stools, with black vinyl cushions. And us, sitting on the stools, at the counter Sipping coffee from our rounded mugs discussing art, theater, and poetry.
All stolen from pictures I've seen,
Interviews I've heard
Biographies I've read.
He was wearing a brown jacket
Thrown on quickly over a wrinkled white shirt,
Most likely worn the day before
I was wearing grey
To cover me in mystery, a mirror to his image
So long I've thought of what I would say,
How I would say it.
But now those dreams run like
Sidewalk chalk in a rainstorm,
And drift down through the sewers that brought them there.
He is a person, not this idea we hold him up to be.
He would not be touched by a
Chance meeting in a hotel lobby
He would not remember me if I wrote him a birthday card.
In all our minds, we cannot separate the job from
The man

His character carries the essence of torment,
The silent mystery that drew us in
Who knows what breaks the silence,
Who has been inside those walls?
None of us that are – why I am ashamed
For in all but the name, I hold him as idol.
Not Idol, never say idol

CATHERINE RIES

Common and Wanting

Around this way it has been lazy days when not running
in the rain
you have soaked through your navy corduroys
strangled bangs hang wet over your forehead
you think about the past over a cup of tea and falling
leaves
emerald green eyes cry with the sadness of cracked
window panes
with soul stains coming out of dirty clothes hampers
so you get out and make your way with haste
but the bicycle with a flat tire stumbles over the
pebbles
on the gravel road that takes you away from people and
ends at the cliff
this would be okay if you weren't so lonely to begin
with
at least your are out of the bedroom with the pictures
you want to make real
there is no way to go back in time to free your mind
when it was actually happening in a way out of your
control
the bike goes unsteady and slow even downhill
the rain starts again and the tire is flat
and the stony road is now uphill
so you stand staring at the sea very still and all
alone
wishing, hoping, praying
for another chance

Catherine Ries

Sign Your Name

Smooth Don Juan walking,
A Greek statue on a platter
Gently soothing my every woe,
Making my hearts protective wall shatter

You intrigue me with your every move,
Your name softly striking a nail in my soul
Wooing me with each step, each gesture,
Breathing soft clouds of tender words as a whole

Eyebrows arched to perfection,
Crowning deep hypnotic eyes
Unmistakable jutting cheekbones above,
Shallow canyons where cheeks should rise

Yet such beauty often makes me doubt,
If I spoke to you, would my words still flow?
Your sacredness comes from a source unknown,
Tu juege me almo ardieno

Catherine Ries

Gema Rodriguez

A Note from the Author

I have been writing poems since fourth grade. I wrote about different things such as nature, animals, love and friendship. But as soon as I entered fifth grade I learned about many different types of poems. My fourth and fifth grade teachers got me excited about expressing myself better by writing about different topics and experiences.

I am a responsible person and earn good grades. Writing is one of the things I love to do. Of course I have a family, my mom's name is Piedad Rodriguez and Ronald Rodriguez is my dad. I also have two brothers named Ronald and the other is Jose Alejandro. I am the middle child.

Cat

I saw a cat,
Wearing a hat
With one gold earring,
Peering through a hole
Of a fence
Riding a Mercedes Benz
The cat wearing a hat,
Parked on a mat
And sat on a rat

Gema Rodriguez

Roses

I have a garden full of roses
They are as beautiful as can be
They are almost as beautiful as me
When my door is open,
Their wonderful smell comes with a breeze
That makes my dog sneeze
So I go outside and sit on a log
And watch the butterflies fly by,
Hear the birds chirping
See the little insects slither
Around in fear
But my roses are still pretty,
As pretty as can be

GEMA RODRIGUEZ

Stephanie Rodriguez

Facts About the Poet

Name: Stephanie Grace Rodriguez
D.O.B: December 22, 1988 @ Miami Beach Florida
Elementary school attended: Sts. Peter and Paul Catholic School
Member of Girls Scout Troop 1575
Member of the school cheerleading team
Member of the school softball team
High School attended: She attended La Salle High School for 9th and 10th grades. She was elected president for her freshman, sophomore, and junior years. Her first year at La Salle she was asked to represent her school, in an ethics convention as well as on the board of students, when La Salle underwent its accreditation. Her sophomore year at La Salle she was also elected the *Homecoming Princess*. That same year, she sent an application to School for Advanced Studies (S.A.S.) where she will be doing her next two years of high school. In those two years she will finish high school and 2 years of college.

Castle in the Sky

Look for me
For I am not that far away
Your eyes are blind and can not see
But your heart will lead the way

The wind will speak to you
And tell you where to go
Open up your mind
And let the feelings grow

A cloud will carry you far away
And your mind will begin to soar
Your body will let go
While your heart will ask for more

Don't ask any questions
Don't even wonder why
There is no purpose
To the Castle in the Sky

STEPHANIE RODRIGUEZ

What it Took

It took a tragedy to end
Lines and barriers betweens friends
All the cries and shouts
There is pain without doubt
It hurts, with all the loss
But no matter how hard it got
Together we fought, why this? Why this now
It's not fair a pain too great not even a country could bare
I still hear it all, all the shouts and cries
People not wanting to die
This is what it took to open our eyes
Now I know why God did this to us
So we'd stop all the fighting, to stop all this fuss
To make us stop and cherish everyday
But, one thing is for sure together we pray
After all the harm is done
We stand together
We stand strong
We go all the way
Because forever we will be the
U S of A

Stephanie Rodriguez

Steven Rodriguez

Steven Rodriguez was born on April 16, 1991 to parents Sergio Rodriguez and Gladys Palacios. He has an older sister Stephanie Rodriguez. His stepfather Marcelo is a part of Steven's family. The family dogs are two Labrador Retrievers named Darwin and Frida.

Steven plays baseball year round. He played with a travelling team for six years and won numerous championships. His most memorable moment was when they walked the player before him and Steven hit a homerun. The game was so close to losing, yet it was saved. On his spare time Steven Rodriguez loves to play baseball and basketball.

Sweat, Not Sweet

Just give me a baseball and bat
Cleats cup and cap
Play hard and sweat
Pitcher throws with a snap
The coach is not sweet
He will make us run
Teaches us discipline
And he thinks it is fun
You can't skip first base to get to home
It is 90 feet to first base
Not making it will be troublesome
Pitching, batting, catching, running
Playing baseball in the hot sun
It is thrilling and exciting
Above all when you hit a homerun
You sweat a lot and get the job done
Great demanding coaches are not sweet
They'll work you hard 'till you sweat
Whether it's cold or in the heat
Bleachers, family, cheering too
As you dive and slide to home base
Then the crowd goes out of control
Sweat and hard plays become quite sweet

Steven Rodriguez

Camila Romero

Camila Romero was born in Havana, Cuba on February 15, 1993. At age five, she came to Miami, Florida with her parents. She is in 7th grade at George Washington Carver Middle School.

Fish

Whenever I see a fish
I make a wish.
Fish is very delish.
Whenever I see one I get ticklish,
and very childish.

Camila Romero

Jonathan Ruano

Jonathan Ruano was born on January 7, 1990 in Miami, Florida. He loves to play basketball and football. He also enjoys eating and working out. His favorite color is baby blue because his eyes are that shade. His most memorable moments were his very first kiss and playing a basketball championship at the Youth Center.

Jonathan is a very friendly easy going person. He loves to relax, talk and hang out with friends and family members. He rarely gets upset about anything or anyone. Those who know Jonathan know that he is a content person. He is currently in high school.

For Your Eyes Only

For your eyes only is my smile for you to see
Together forever we will always be
For your eyes only the letters that I write
We will make up every time we fight
Hold hands gently and talk till it is dark
For your eyes only the presents that I give
For all eternity for as long as we live

JONATHAN RUANO

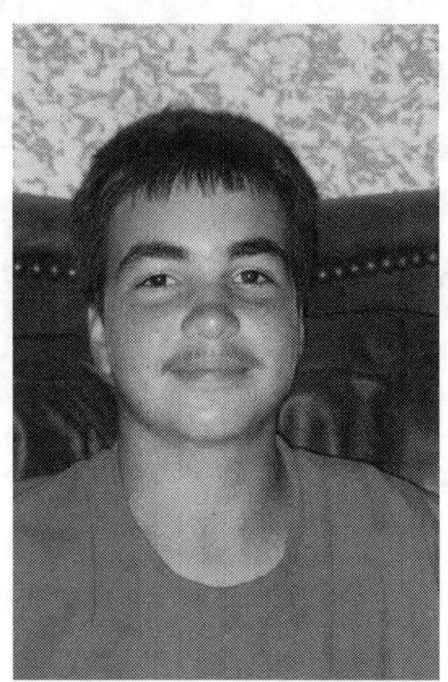

Justin Ruano

Justin Ruano is Jonathan's younger brother. Both brothers share the same two parents Roger Ruano and Mabel Ruano. Justin was born on July 29, 1992 in Miami, Florida. He loves playing basketball and video games. His favorite subject is mathematics. He also enjoys going to the movies. His peak experience was when he broke his wrist because it was very painful.

Cousins

What do cousins mean to me?
Love, care, play and fun
With or without glasses you can see
Eating hamburgers with or without a bun
When we are together we have a blast
Spending time with cousins each and every day
Riding your bicycle – going fast
Also during holidays and during my birthday
We sing and laugh
PlayStation 2
Play basketball and act like fools
We also hide and scare each other, "BOO!"

Justin Ruano

Megan Ruiz

A Note from the Author

Hi my name is Megan Ruiz. I am 11 years old and I have two brothers, one older and one younger. I go to Saint Timothy Parish School, in Miami, Florida. I am in 6th grade.

My hobbies are playing basketball, softball, soccer, volleyball and chatting online. I like a lot of different genres of music, such as rap, R & B, regeton and many more. Now you know a little about me.

My Love

My love is awesome,
My love is cool,
My love is a basketball,
That boy was such a fool.

He thought he could beat me,
I'd like to see him try,
My love has got my back,
I bet that boy would cry.

My love is always there,
All that boy had left was a prayer,
A prayer he could beat a girl,
Please, I'm faster than a squirrel.

MEGAN RUIZ

So Many

I have so many friends,
They are all so great,
My faith in them never bends.
I love them,
They love me,
They truly are my gem.
We talk on the phone,
We chat on line,
I'm pretty sure that's a good sign.
My friends and I have great times together,
I count each as one of my blessings,
We will be together forever.

MEGAN RUIZ

Something Else

It was something else.
Incredible!
We were having a party,
The neighbors were here,
We were having fun,
Wasn't it supposed to be a category 1?

It must have been a mistake,
There were trees flying, rain falling and wind blowing.
Hopeless!
The power was gone and it was hot,
We didn't know how long it would be
It seemed endless, at least to me.

Three long days.
Disasterous!
No TV, no music, No computer
What were we suppose to do?
Board games, playing outside, in the pool.
We survived.

The power is back.
Finally!
We were in AC, we have TV,
Now we see it wasn't so bad for us,
We pray for those in need.

Megan Ruiz

Jorge Sanz

Jorge Sanz was born on March 19, 1993 in Miami, Florida. His parents' names are Jorge and Aimee Sanz. George is the older of two brothers. His brother's name is Alejandro Sanz.

Georgie enjoys playing football and basketball, watching and playing a variety of sports, listening to music, dancing, playing video games and hanging out with his friends. He loves attending Gulliver. He can also not get enough of vacations to Orlando with his immediate family, uncles, grandparents and cousins.

Jorge Sanz (Georgie, George) has earned awards and achievements such as making the Dean's list at school, football pop Warner championship, basketball Y.M.C.A. championship and Physical Fitness Award. His future goals are: winning state championship for high school football, and playing in the NFL.

Katrina's Fury

The hurricane is hitting
No lights, no TV.
In the dark hallways
I can barely see.
And our huge oak tree
Will never again be
Rain pounding on the windows,
Trees falling to the ground
No air-conditioning, no power
So it's hot hour after hour.
The wind is strong
For way too long
The leaves fill the pool
The next day there will be no school.
Sitting around bored,
Hoping time flies by.
Waiting what tomorrow brings to us,
Hopefully Miami isn't in chaos.

JORGE SANZ

Alfredo Toll

A Note from the Author

My name is Alfredo Luis Toll. I am ten years old. I have a big brother that is 18, a mother that is 41 and a dad that is 46 years old. We were all born in Havana, Cuba. When I grow up I want to become a doctor like my mom because my mom told me that it feels good when you save somebody's life. My favorite food is Cuban food like rice, steak, beans, pork, congris and yucca.

When I Grow Up

When I grow up and become a doctor
Many young and old lives I will save
My mom says it feels so good to make a difference
Using the talents that my life gave

When I grow up I might become president
My teacher always would say
I am popular, love to smile and talk a lot
I am persuasive and usually get my way

When I grow up I will be somebody important
I will work hard and try my best
I will go to college and will do homework
Will also study hard to pass every test

Alfredo Toll

Laurence Tommasi

A Note from the Author

My name is Laurence Philip Tommasi, Jr. My parents are Laurence Philip Tommasi, Sr. and Liana Lima Tommasi. I am the oldest of two brothers. My brother's name is Joseph Andrew Tommasi. I was born in Miami, Florida and I am 13 years old. I have attended Saints Peter and Paul Catholic School since kindergarten. I finished 7th grade in the honor roll last year and I will be starting 8th grade on August 8, 2005.

I have attended semi-private drawing and painting classes for the past two years. Last year, I won 1st Place in my school's Art Show. I look forward to graduation this year and starting high school the following year. My goal is to one day become a graphic designer.

Danny Let It Rip

Danny thought he was so hip,
But when he walked in, he let it rip.
When he went outside, he saw a moose.
But when he went back in, he let it loose.
Danny thought he was having fun.
But the next day, he let out of the big one.
Danny Olsen was so shy.
Because when he let it out, the birds went bye, bye.
He went to the restaurant and bought a milkshake.
But when he went back home, he caused an earthquake.

LAURENCE PHILIP TOMMASI
(Larry Tommasi)

Alexandra Varona

Alexandra Gladys Varona was born on April 7, 1988 in Miami, Florida. She is currently an International Baccalaureate Program Diploma Candidate at Coral Gables High School in Coral Gables, Florida from which she will graduate in May of 2006. In her spare time, Alex, as her friends call her, enjoys reading (her favorites include the Harry Potter series and essays on the subject of psychology) and spending time with her friends and family. Alex is at this time anticipating acceptance into the University of Florida after her involvement in the Hispanic High School Scholars Program. She plans to study dentistry at the university with aspirations of specializing within the field.

The following literary piece was written when Alexandra was in the eighth grade. She earned the "Pride" 2002 Middle School Writing Portfolio Competition, acknowledging her as a runner-up. A certificate was awarded recognized by the Miami-Dade County Public Schools for a distinguished portfolio initiative and distinction in education. To this day the tie between family, friends, teachers and students remain. The bond shall continue through eternity.

Eighth Grade Essay

I remember it like it was yesterday. Second grade was dreadfully mind numbing. Fourth grade was awfully tedious. But, the memory of third grade was, and is still the most vivid of them all. My best school year would indisputably have to be third grade on account of all the new experiences it gave me, my teacher, and the fact that it was the year I met my best friend.

To begin, people grow and alter after gaining new experiences. To me, third grade was a milestone. In my previous school, Silver Bluff Elementary advancing to third grade meant one gained more "special" privileges. For example, it was the first year I went to the "Dade County Youth Fair" with the school and many other field trips the underclassmen weren't given a chance to experience. It also meant that my parents trusted me more by letting me go by myself. From these expeditions I learned a lot about myself and taking responsibility for my own actions while learning to be more independent. Third grade was also a very important year for me because I grew as a person. Teachers now expected even more of me. They anticipated one hundred and ten percent. I was projected to act more maturely and be a role model for the underclassmen.

As a result, I became more established and trustworthy. For instance, I was given more difficult assignments and teachers became stricter. Being a third grader gave me a sense of courage. This empowered me to enter numerous contests and participate more in school. For example, I entered the talent show and won first place along with my three closest friends for portraying the "Spice Girls", my favorite group of singers back then. As a result, this made me more fearless and encouraged me to try new things.

Furthermore, teachers play a major role in the bringing up of a child. They're almost like second mothers or fathers. They see everything our actual parents can't and then report back! It happens every year, in the beginning I always dislike my teachers, but slowly and surely I grow to love them, making it harder to advance to the next year. Mrs. Monnar was exceptional! From the moment I entered her class that sunny day in September, I knew I would enjoy the third grade. I walked in and the look on my face gave away my true feelings. I was utterly petrified!

Mrs. Monnar immediately noticed and came rushing to my assistance. She took me aside and assured me I would be loved and comforted in her class. What intrigued me the most about Mrs. Monnar was her style of teaching; how she could teach us so much and yet we never grew bored and always yearned for more. She made me aware of poetry and the affect it has on a person. Because of her, I grew to love it and became a novice poet! She introduced me to Shel Silverstein, my favorite poet. Mrs. Monnar was also sort of an activist for reading. She encouraged me to read and enjoy it. She taught us to look at it as something I wanted to do, not something I was required to do. Soon, it became a hobby; something I set a side time for in my hectic schedule.

Moreover, school would not be the same if I didn't have a best friend to experience it with. Third grade was an exception because it was the year I met my best friend, Sarah, who I still know to this day. Mrs. Monnar paired us up to do a book report on a book we were all reading as a class. At first, we were both very uncomfortable with the aspect of working together due to the fact that we had never really met before. But soon enough, I found her to be interesting and trustworthy. We suddenly just clicked! It was almost like a cosmic bond we had created. At that controversial time in my life I needed someone who was going through the same changes I was going through. We understood one another.

It all started when I came to her for condolence. I was upset at my older sister for treating me badly. She comforted my by telling me what I could do to let my sister know that she was making me feel this way since she had an older sister too and could relate to what I was going through. I would, in turn, assist her with her math homework since I was getting better marks in the subject. Of course we worked marvelously together and received an "A" on our report. From then on, we were inseparable!

Consequently, all these things and more combined made third grade the best school year of my life! It was my best school year due to all the new experiences it gave me, my teacher, and the fact that it was the year I met my best friend. If only all school years were as enjoyable as this one was!

Alexandra Varona

Kristin Vazquez

A Note from the Author

My name is Kristin Vazquez. I was born in Miami, Florida. I have two sisters named Vanessa and Alexandra. My favorite sports are cross-country and track and field.

Angel

An Angel God has called home today
Much to our sadness and dismay
He lived on Earth 4 short years
But brought so much joy and happy tears
As we say goodbye and set him free
Let's never forget how precious life can be.

Kristin Vazquez

Leidy and Linda Villa

About the Authors

Leidy and Linda are identical twins. They were born in Miami, Florida on March 26, 1996. Both girls like to run, play tag and spend time with their brothers Diego and Daniel. They also have many other things in common that they share a love for. For example, they love their cats. They also hope to study for the same careers. Leidy and Linda love vacationing with their family especially when they go to Georgia, U.S.A. where they have cousins and Medellin, Colombia, South America where they have family from their mother's side.

Identical Twins

Being twins is so much fun
We can be sneaky sometimes
In the darkness and under the sun
Trying our best to get dimes
When she fails a mission
It is up to me
To do a trick like a magician
Then we both flee
We are always together
We get on each others' nerves
Sometimes we bug each other
While eating strawberry preserves
We are identical twins
By loving us
Family wins

LEIDY AND LINDA VILLA

Chantelle Viloria

Chantelle Viloria was born on October 4, 1995 in Miami, Florida. She has a younger brother who lives in Santo Domingo. Chantelle enjoys music, art and computer classes. She also enjoys playing tag plus hide-and-seek in her backyard with her cousins. Chantelle wants to become a music teacher when she grows up.

The Haunted House

Once upon a time there were two sisters in the same class. One of those two sisters was me. We were playing in school when suddenly a boy came yelling, "There is a haunted house!" We ran out to take a look at the house.

It was a huge deserted mansion. The door was cracked and the windows were broken. It definitely looked scary. After looking from the outside and walking to our home, we asked our parents if we could go inside the haunted house. The agreed but asked us to be very careful. We said, "Yes!" excitedly.

We packed our things for our trip. We wanted to stay there an entire week. So mom packed our lunch boxes with enough food two last for seven days. She also packed enough clothing for us. Mom even gave us a good luck charm and a good-bye kiss as we left.

My sister and I were so excited about our adventure. This trip was going to turn into an exciting journey. I could feel it in my bones. We finally arrived and we both went inside the deserted mansion. It was very dark and dusty inside.

This haunted house was almost too creepy to lie down and get a good night sleep. My sister and I decided to sleep in the same room. We slept one right next to the other and we must have been so tired that we snoozed and probably snored through the whole night.

When we woke up the next morning, we ate breakfast and thought we heard some strange noises but it was nothing. All of a sudden my sister and I saw a skeleton. As it fell into the room, the skeleton mysteriously just moved back up and disappeared into the ceiling. "Ahhh!" we screamed.

One day of this creepy visit was enough. We decided that it would be the last day that we would spend in that strange mansion. It was scary and fun at the same time. I guess everybody likes some excitement from time to time.

Finally we packed up and decided to go home. We told our parents about the exciting and creepy experience. We both told mom and dad about the strange noises, spine-chilling skeleton, the fun, excitement, screaming and being scared. However, we weren't too scared; because we saw the boy who told us about the haunted house hanging out around the outside of the deserted mansion.

Chantelle Viloria

Denise Washington

Denise was born in Hollywood, Florida on May 9, 1989. She is the daughter of Esther Farmer, officer for the City of Miami Police Dept. She currently attends New World School of the Arts where her focus is vocal music. Her main career goal is to become a professional jazz singer and possibly own her own jazz club. Her previous achievements have ranged from sports to music to educational awards. She has a passion for jazz music and studies it at New World also. She is the singer for her high school's jazz band which has won 1st place in probably the most competitive competition among nationwide bands in New York called Essentially Ellington. She has two more years of high school and after that she plans to attend a college in New York, preferably Juilliard School, New York University, Berklee College of Music in Mass., or University of Miami in her hometown Miami, Florida.

Midnight Hour Blues

Blue days seem to haunt me
And depress me
May say I'm crazy but what,
What will I do
Now that I'm so blue
My midnight hour blues

Could it be the man I loved left me
Could it be a conclusion of my burdens
Could it be a distraction from reality
Oh Lord help me with these blues days
Bring back all my happy days

'Cause I'm lonely
Want somebody
But have nobody
To care for still I found a way
To proceed each day
I drink tears for food
My midnight hour blues

DENISE WASHINGTON
** Actually a song that I wrote. Was originally a poem**

To the Fast Babies

Slow yo role young one,
There's so much you can miss.
So much for you to learn,
So much more time for this.

Slow yo role young child,
Cause that's all you really are.
You're not yet an adult,
You haven't come that far.

Slow yo role young body,
Don't dress to make it look old.
Don't treat yourself like trash,
Treat yourself like precious gold.

Slow yo role young mind,
And learn all you can.
Don't put off education,
To go looking for no man

Slow yo role young baby,
Enjoy your youth while it's fresh.
I want you to grow and live,
I want you to have success.

Denise Washington

Si Tu Savais

(If You Knew)

Ah! *Si tu savais*
How I wonder about you.
Wondering if you wonder about me
How I remember you under that willow tree.

Oh! *Si tu savais*
How I remember the effect you gave.
Without a touch, you delivered.
Memories so nice to make me quiver

Oo! *Si tu savais*
How I cried at your good bye.
Wondering was this all a joke,
And just another harmless lie

Hm! *Si tu savais*
How mad you make me feel.
Finding out the duplicity of your game
Anger built up enough to kill.

Well *Si tu savais*
How much I'm over you
How nice it was while it lasted
But you weren't genuinely true

DENISE WASHINGTON

Matthew Williams

Matthew Williams is the son of Patricia Williams and beloved City of Miami Police Officer William Williams who died in the line of duty. Matthew is a senior at Coral Gables Senior High School. He started writing poems in his early high school years. Matthew is friendly, kind and loveable. He enjoys spending time with family and friends. Matthew is in the school's varsity football team and also plays football in community teams.

Football

Someone rugged, yet gentle
Makes a football player
Running, wrestling, leaping
At times warming up the bleacher
Musky smelling locker room
Heart and family
Lots of dedication
Practice, practice, practice
Drenched in sweat front and back
Hard helmet
Tackle, fumble
Groaning noises uh, uh
I am a football player
Football is the game
To play and watch
Whether wild or tame

Matthew Williams

Ibrain Rey Zirini

Ibrain Rey Zirini is a student at a La Salle High School in Miami, Florida. He is the younger brother of Melissa-Marie Zirini. From a very young age, he expressed interest and talent in the arts, especially in writing short stories and poetry. He enjoys drawing, animating and playing video games. Ibrain hopes to go into computer animation for games and movies. Ibrain's imaginative stories will surely entertain audiences in the future.

The Moon's Glare

Though you have gone
And I have stayed
This is what I've made
A vision of you in my head

Though you are there
And I am here
I feel you close
For the moon I see
Stares back at you

Ibrain Zirini

Pet

Sweet creature of darkness
I see you there weeping
I'll take you in as my own
Young pup, your eyes tell sadness
Your scars tell stories
I'll be there for you, so don't you weep
My small friend, I'll be us two
Forever, you and me

Ibrain Zirini

Resources

Web Ring

Poetry from Planet Earth Web Ring
http://www.readersareleadersusa.net/links.html

Helpful Web sites

Academy of American Poets
http://www.poets.org/

Clipart.com
More than 6 million clipart images, photos, illustrations, animations, fonts and sounds available to use from Clipart.com content. Thanks to clipart.com, the pictures and illustrations were made possible for the writers from the "Past" included in this anthology.
http://www.clipart.com/

Inkwater Press
Inkwater Press is focused on distinctive quality design and production. Offering standard design and production services; Inkwater Press is a book-loving publisher. The expert staff will produce your print-on-demand book making your dream of seeing your literary work published come true.
http://www.inkwaterpress.com/

Poems and Letters about Adoption
http://thelaboroflove.com/prose/adoption.html

Poetryteachers.com
Poetryteachers.com is a great site for teachers, learners and parents who love poetry.
http://www.poetryteachers.com/

RhymeZone
Find rhymes, synonyms, definitions, and more:http://www.rhymezone.com/

Custom Web site designs by Tammie.
www.diamondwebsites.com

Mother, Teacher, Writer

Ana Monnar

analovestoread@msn.com
www.ReadersAreLeadersUSA.net

EDUCATION:

December 8, 1981	Florida International University Degree: Master of Science in Elementary Education
December 17, 1977	Florida International University Degree: Bachelor of Science in Childhood Education
May 1975	Miami-Dade Community College Degree: Associate in Arts

CERTIFICATION

Certificate Type	Professional Active
Subject Coverage	E.S.O.L. Endorsement Early Childhood Elementary Education

EXPERIENCES

July 2001
to the Present

Fourth Grade Teacher/Multiple Intelligences
E.H. Mainstreaming,
Learning Disabled
Gifted
Regular Education
E.S.O.L. Students

July 1998
to June 2001

Title I Reading Leader

August 1996
to June 1998

Third Grade Honors/Academic Excellence Teacher

September 1995
to June 1996

Chapter I Reading Curriculum Specialist

November 1993
to September 1995

Chapter I Math Curriculum Specialist

September 1993
to November 1993

Chapter I Resource Teacher

March 1980
to August 1993

Second Grade Teacher

JOB ASSIGNMENTS / DUTIES / RESPONSIBILITIES

2002- to Present Grade Level Chairperson
Fourth Grade Teacher/Multiple Intelligences
Reading Leader (Three Years)
School Ambassador 1998-99 & 1999-2000 (Two Years)
Reading Curriculum Specialist (One Year)
Math Curriculum Specialist (Two Years)
Title I Resource Teacher
E.S.O.L. Self-contained Teacher
Third Grade Honors/Academic Excellence Teacher
Peer Teacher (Ten Times)
Grade-Level Chairperson (Three Years)
Provided Workshops for Parents, Teachers, Administrators
America Reads Coordinator for Silver Bluff Elementary (Three Years)
Participant in Child Study Team, Staffing, Student Performance Plan, Pupil Progression Plan
Promote/Encourage/Support Comprehensive Reading Plan (C.R.P.)
Young Authors, Books with Wings, Theodore Gibson Oratorical Project, Miami International Book Fair Sponsor in the School Site Level

ACCOMPLISHMENTS

Featured on Channel 23 Univision, Adoption Interview, November 2003
Miami Herald, Neighbors Section, Super Teacher, November 27, 2003
Author of:

Half Full, Or Half Empty?: A Collection of Poems Written by Ana Monnar
Poetry from Planet Earth
Gold and Glitter
Relax: New and Selected Poems
Adoption? Thank God for That Option!
The Law of the Funnel
It Doesn't Matter
Hungry Woman
Heart of Stone
Clutter

Successful Grant Proposals

1999-2000	WLRN Ready to Learn Proposal
1998-99	WLRN Ready to Learn Proposal
1995-96	The Citibank Success Fund Learning with Themes
1996	Dade Public Education fund Mini-Grant Cooperative Learning with Unifix Cubes
1995	Title II Eisenhower Grant Linking Mathematics to Literature
1995	Mathematics Teacher of the Year Nominee
1994	Science Teacher of the Year Nominee
1988	Teacher of the Year

Looking for Writers from Around the World of All Ages, Creed and Color

Express Yourself 101 SERIES

- Please submit your literary piece written in the English language.
- Works may be on any topic as long as it is geared towards all ages.
- Up to three original poems, lyrics and/or short stories, a picture of the writer and a biography (one to two paragraphs) sent via e-mail.
- Submitting work that is not yours is against the law and it is plagiarism. By submitting poems, short stories, lyrics, pictures and information about the author; you are agreeing that Readers Are Leaders U.S.A. may reproduce in print and/or post on the Web site.
- Please make sure you sign and mail permission agreement. Your rights will go back to you. Returning authors are welcomed as long as the poems are different from the previous submission.
- Once your literary piece is selected based on merit, an agreement form will be e-mailed for you to sign and mail to the address that will be provided.
- There is no obligation to buy any copies of the book.
- Readers Are Leaders U.S.A., Inc. has the right to revise the rules...
- You may wish to submit your poetry, lyrics and/or short story for consideration to publication in print in an anthology and/or Web site.
- If your work is selected…
- Provide contact information to readers (Brief Biography, Web site URL, Title(s) of previously published book(s), (self-published, print on demand, traditional, or if not applicable leave blank)
- FREE; no entry fees – Your copyrights revert back to you.
- You earn no royalties, just recognition and a chance to see your work in print.
- Your submission must be your own original work that you own sole rights to.
- You must be 18 or over, or have parent sign a consent agreement.
- I hereby certify that the above poems, lyrics and/or short stories are my original work and that all rights to the literary pieces are mine and belong to me.

- I understand that my poems, lyrics and/or short story if selected will be published in an anthology as my original work and under my own copyright by Readers Are Leaders U.S.A.

analovestoread@msn.com
http://www.ReadersAreLeadersUSA.net

Readers Are Leaders U.S.A. does not assume responsibility to verify the authorship of each literary work. Each and every writer confirmed that the literary work submitted to be their own original work and that they have sole ownership of each piece.

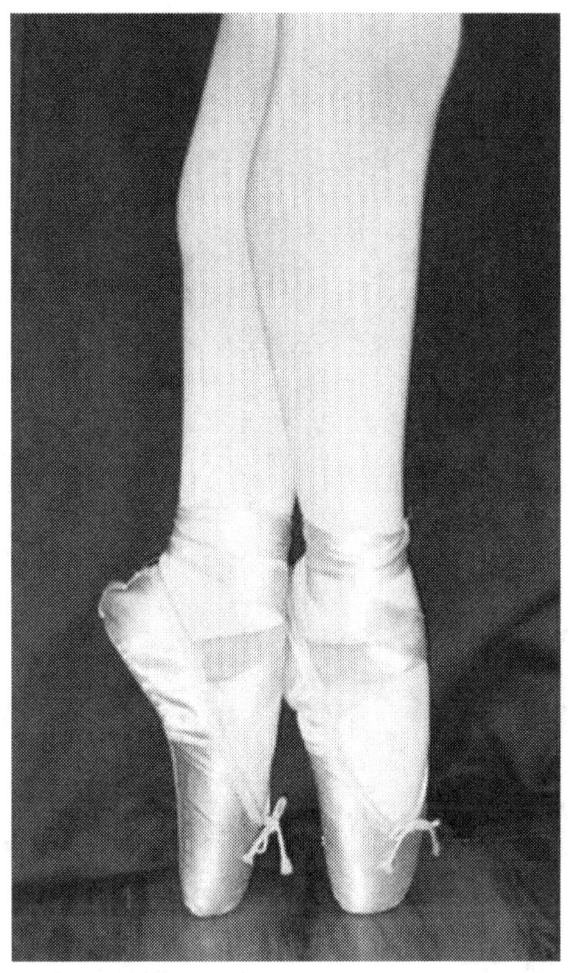

This picture was captured by Ana Monnar, mother and it is her daughter Anna Lee Monnar at age nine standing on point. The setting is at **Maria Verdeja School of the Arts** *where Anna attended from age four to the time she finished fifth grade. Middle school participation in sports such as basketball, softball, volleyball, cross-country, plus track-and field took countless hours. The many years of dance helped Anna's endurance and grace in other areas.*

Index of Poem Titles

Index of Writers

A

B

C

D

M

O

P

Q

R

S

www.ingramcontent.com/pod-product-compliance
Lightning Source LLC
Chambersburg PA
CBHW060604310726
48982CB00008B/1237/J

* 9 7 8 0 9 7 6 8 0 3 5 2 2 *